# Terrific Tips

## FOR TODDLER TEACHERS

**By Gayle Bittinger, Mary Ann Hodge, and Jenny Cooper Rose**
**Illustrated by Priscilla Burris**

**Totline® Publications**
A Division of Frank Schaffer Publications, Inc.
Torrance, California

Totline® Publications would like to acknowledge the following child-care professionals for contributing some of the activities in this book: Silvana Clark, Bellingham, WA; Neoma Coale, Ontario, CA; Karen Focht, Reading, PA; Lisa Fransen, Tucson, AZ; Paula Laughtland, Edmonds, WA; Ruth Prall, Sterling, CO; Vicki Reynolds, East Hanover, NJ; Karen Seehusen, Fort Dodge, IA; Betty Silkunas, Lansdale, PA; Diane Thom, Maple Valley, WA; Mary Ulrich, Gilbertsville, PA; Margaret S. White, Issaquah, WA.

**Managing Editor:** Kathleen Cubley
**Contributing Editors:** Carol Gnojewski, Susan Hodges,
    Elizabeth McKinnon, Susan Sexton, Jean Warren
**Copyeditor:** Kris Fulsaas
**Proofreader:** Miriam Bulmer
**Editorial Assistant:** Durby Peterson
**Graphic Designer (Interior):** Sarah Ness
**Layout Artist:** Gordon Frazier
**Graphic Designer (Cover):** Brenda Mann Harrison
**Production Manager:** Melody Olney

*Terrific Tips for Toddler Teachers* is a compilation and revision of these Totline Publications materials: WPH 4013 *Classroom Management*; WPH 4014 *Discovery Play*; WPH 4015 *Dramatic Play*; WPH 4016 *Large Motor Play*; WPH 4017 *Small Motor Play*; and WPH 4018 *Word Play*.

ISBN: 1-57029-237-X
Library of Congress Catalog Card Number 98-60801

Printed in the United States of America
Published by Totline Publications

Business Office: 23740 Hawthorne Blvd.
                Torrance, CA 90505

# Contents

# Classroom Management

# Scheduling Tips

**1** Develop a plan or a schedule for your toddlers' day. They gain a sense of security from knowing what will happen and when. Children who operate all day without a schedule often become bored or difficult to handle. When deciding on a schedule, be sure to consider the basic needs of your children.

**2** Young children need nourishment on a regular basis—about every 1½ to 2 hours. Plan your children's other activities and naptime around this need.

**3** Plan to offer toddlers water regularly. It is wise to schedule water breaks, particularly after an outdoor playing time. Many young children do not have the verbal skills to request water. Scheduled water breaks ensure that they have access to the water they need.

**4** Rest is another vital part of a toddler's schedule. Most young children take one nap a day after lunch. Make sure that the time before naptime is relaxing and quiet. Plan a pre-nap ritual, including a bathroom visit, so your children are able to make the transition more easily.

**5** Write in bathroom breaks or time for potty training. Children learn more easily and quickly if bathroom breaks are regular and consistent. Plan on having bathroom breaks every 1½ to 2 hours.

**6** Schedule some outdoor play for every day. Even if the weather is very hot or very cold, toddlers need at least some time outside. If you have extreme weather, try to plan your outdoor time when the temperature is at its most comfortable, early morning for hot summer days and afternoons in the winter.

**7** Allow time for getting dressed to go outside, especially when it is cold and snowing. Consider this time to be a learning period. Encourage your children to be as independent as possible when putting on their coats, boots, hats, mittens, and so on. You may want to arrange to have one teacher inside and one teacher outside, so that as soon as a child is bundled up, he or she may go outside instead of getting too warm inside waiting for others to put on their outdoor gear.

**8** Build in time for rituals when your children arrive in the morning and leave in the afternoon. Make sure that you are able to greet them individually and help them separate from their parents if they need it. Saying goodbye to each child as he or she leaves is also important.

**9** Consider the ratio of active to quiet activities in your children's day. Try to alternate these throughout the day. Be sure to leave some larger blocks of time for self-directed activities, such as table toys, large motor play, dramatic play, and so on. Toddlers especially need time to watch, join, explore, practice, and then learn.

**10** Write your schedule in large print where everyone can see it. A written schedule helps parents understand what their children are doing throughout the day, and it helps keep you on track. Of course, schedules are only guides. You must still be aware of your children and their interests and the need for flexibility. The schedule may say it is time for stories and songs, but not every toddler in the room must be sitting and involved. It is important to allow children to participate as they are able.

# Records and Lesson Plans

**1** A good toddler program uses effective record keeping. There is a variety of information you must know. Have parents fill out a registration form before their child's first day. The form should include such information as complete name of toddler, parents' names and places of employment, emergency names and phone numbers, age and birthdate of child, allergies, food likes and dislikes, and general health. You may ask for other information such as developmental needs of the child and successful comforting techniques. Provide any forms your licensing agency requires you to have, such as immunization records.

**2** Be aware that the information that a parent gives you is confidential. Store all original records in a safe and secured place.

**3** You will probably want to keep each child's emergency information available to you quickly at all times. You may want to photocopy this information and keep it on a clipboard. Hang the clipboard inside a cupboard that can be locked. This way, the information is easily accessible and kept private.

**4** Design a log for keeping track of daily information for each child. This should include information about the child's eating, sleeping, and eliminating. A part of this form could also be a short report of the activities of the day. What did the child enjoy doing? Were any developmental milestones reached today? Did he or she get hurt?

**5** Chart the developmental progress of each child in your care. This information can show areas where a child needs a little extra help. It also helps for planning activities, and it is useful for parent conferences.

**6** To keep track of your toddlers' developmental progress, you can begin by keeping anecdotal records. These are records where you write your comments about what a child did on a particular day. Be sure that all of these notes are dated and initialed and filed away in a special place. Later, when you compile each child's notes, you will be able to see the progression of his or her skills.

**7** Another way to chart developmental progress is to use a simple developmental checklist. The checklist would list a variety of developmental milestones in several different skill areas, such as large motor, small motor, social, self-help, language, and cognitive. Go through the checklist every three or four months for each child. Do not expect all toddlers to be able to do all of the items on the report. Two or three progress reports shown to a child's parents at conference time can remind everyone of how much the child has grown.

**8** Write lesson plans in advance and post them in your room. Traditional lesson plan forms are not appropriate for toddlers, so you will have to devise your own.

**9** Lesson plans for toddlers would include several activities in three or four different developmental areas. There would be enough ideas to be stimulating, but the plans would also take into consideration the need toddlers have for repetition and practice.

**10** Change your toddler lesson plans on a weekly basis rather than a daily basis. On Monday some children will be hesitant to participate, but by Friday they will have mastered the activity because they have had the opportunity to practice it all week.

# Selecting Furniture

**4** When selecting chairs, choose ones with a wide base so they will not tip over easily. Chairs that are only 8 inches off the floor are best for toddlers—when they sit on them their feet can touch the floor. It is also nice to have chairs with arms or sides on them to help toddlers sit securely in them. Make sure you have a chair for each child in your group.

**5** Choose a table that is large enough for your children to sit around without feeling crowded. The table should also be the right height, reaching about midchest on the seated toddler.

**1** Look for furniture that is well made. Sturdy furniture can take a lot of moving by young children and will not break when knocked over. It can be climbed onto and into without collapsing or tipping over. It should not fall apart when it is used in ways it was not designed for.

**2** Second-hand furniture is not the best choice for this age group. Safety is such an important issue and toddlers are hard on furniture. It is worthwhile to invest in new furniture, made to current safety codes, that will last.

**3** Make sure that wooden furniture has a smooth, durable finish that will not splinter. When selecting plastic furniture, it must be heavy-duty plastic that will not crack or break.

**6** Discard baby furniture, such as highchairs and cribs. Toddlers are taking many steps toward independence and the furniture around them should reflect that. However, preschool furniture is too big for toddlers. Many companies now offer a selection of toddler-size furniture that is just right.

**7** Select furniture that you can keep clean. Upholstered fabric, fancy scrollwork, and porous materials are difficult to sanitize.

**8** Make sure you have shelves for the toys that allow your children to access them without reaching over their heads or climbing.

**9** Many programs have an adult rocking chair in the toddler room. Before adding one to your room, consider these two disadvantages. First, a rocking chair takes up a lot of space that could be used in other ways. Second, a rocking chair encourages relaxing and observing instead of the more important tasks of interacting with your children by kneeling on the floor with them, reading books to them in the book area, or sitting with them at the table.

**10** If you are able, plan for sinks in your room that are low enough for your toddlers to reach without climbing on stools. This makes hand washing so much easier and gives them a wonderful feeling of independence.

# Room Arrangements

**1** Planning your toddler room requires more than putting a few pieces of furniture and a bunch of toys in a room. The room must be large enough for your children to play in without bumping into each other and the furniture. When the environment is inadequate because the room is too small or the furniture is poorly arranged, disciplinary problems are more common and everyone is unhappy. Take the time to find the right balance for your room and your toddlers.

**2** Make sure your room has a large area with a carpet. Toddlers fall down easily and a cushioned floor makes for a softer landing. They also like to sit down and play on a floor that is warm and comfortable.

**3** Use the shelves and furniture in the room to create little "rooms" where your children can play. Designate each of these rooms as a different play area. One easy way to have enough furniture and shelves to create all these rooms is to place the furniture or shelves in arrangements other than against the walls.

**4** Use the play center approach that is common in preschool settings. Arrange toys and supplies on open shelves in the areas where the children play with them. Children should be able to take a toy from a shelf and immediately play with it.

**5** When you set up play areas, try to arrange the quiet areas in one part of the room and the noisy, active areas in another part.

**9** Keep a high shelf or other teacher-only area for storing materials that must be used with adult supervision. Items in this area can include scissors, paint, and some manipulatives.

**10** Strive to find the optimal amount between too many and too few toys on your shelves. If you have too many, children have a tendency to just dump them on the floor. If you have too few, sharing becomes the problem. When children are happy and playing independently and not clearing off the shelves, a balance has been attained.

**6** Keep play centers open for your toddlers to play in throughout the day, except while eating and sleeping.

**7** Some areas require more room than others. For instance, the large muscle skills area needs more space than the book corner.

**8** Set aside an area where your children can hang their coats and other personal items. Each toddler needs to have his or her own hook or cubby. Sharing is just too difficult at this age.

# Arranging Play Centers

**1** Select items for your children to play with that will help them learn and explore their world. The items you select should reflect their age and the world in which they live.

**2** Set up your home life center with a toddler-size stove, a shelf for some dishes, doll beds, dolls, and a table with chairs.

**3** Keep the book area stocked with a variety of books. Board books are the sturdiest for this age group. Have books available to your children at all times to encourage a love of books and reading.

**4** Having an area for water or sand play is messy and often requires a lot of cleanup, but the benefits your children receive from this tactile center is well worth the effort.

**5** Toddlers need table toys to help them develop their small motor and coordination skills. These toys include large interlocking blocks, building blocks, and other toys to put together.

**6** Include a climbing structure and a few riding toys in your large muscle skills area. Push and pull toys are important as well. This area is also a great place for large, lightweight blocks, such as homemade box blocks.

**7** Set up an art center with paper, crayons, and other safe, creative materials. On occasion, supervise the art center so you can have out additional art materials, such as scissors or tape, that require adult assistance or guidance.

**8** Think about having a variety of hard and soft items in the room. Hard items are easy to provide—a climber, some blocks, a table and chairs. Soft items are a little more difficult, but it is important to have washable stuffed animals in your room, along with pillows to sit or lie on while relaxing or reading books.

**9** Because toddlers engage in parallel play (playing side by side) rather than cooperative play (playing together), conflicts can arise when two or more children want to play with the same toy at once. To keep these conflicts to a minimum, purchase popular toys in bulk. It is easier to have five identical dump trucks than five vehicles of different styles and colors.

**10** Set up a science area where your toddlers can safely explore a variety of natural objects. Clear-plastic bottles with items that sink or float, a nonbreakable magnifying glass to look through, and large magnets and a nonaluminum baking sheet are all possibilities.

# Communicating With Parents

**3** Include community events on your bulletin board. Your parents will appreciate knowing about a special storytime on Saturday or a puppet show scheduled at the community college. (Make sure the information is current, though. It is frustrating to find out about an exciting event *after* it has taken place.)

**4** Send home copies of the words to the songs you are singing with the toddlers. This way, parents can help their toddlers sing and share the songs at home.

**5** Make simple activity packets to take home. The packets could have sewing cards, three-piece puzzles, or matching games in them for the toddlers and their parents to do together.

**1** Put a bulletin board outside your room. Post your lesson plans for the week and any other information you would like parents to know. Keep the information current, so parents will want to be sure to check the board regularly.

**2** On your bulletin board, designate which information is important. Have a section with the heading "High Priority" or "You'll Want to Know This."

**8** Reassure parents that any questions or concerns they have are legitimate and that you want the opportunity to answer them. Make an appointment to talk over the phone or to meet for a quick conference.

**9** Encourage parents to observe or volunteer in the classroom. Even an occasional 30 minutes gives parents a new perspective on their child's day.

**10** Each week or month, send home a simple one-page or even half-page newsletter that tells parents about what has been happening in your room. Write about what your children have been studying and the skills they have been developing or strengthening.

**6** Write a simple parent-child activity calendar for each week or month of the year. Provide easy activities parents and children can do together in the morning or evening, such as singing a song or touching their toes five times.

**7** Assemble a photo album depicting a typical day in your classroom. Allow newly enrolled parents to take the photo album home to share with their toddler before he or she starts in your room. Children are more comfortable on their first day if they know a little bit about what to expect.

# Keeping Your Room Clean

**1** Practice stringent hygiene in your toddler room. Washing hands is the single most important activity you can do to promote sanitation. Teach your children how to wash their hands. Help them sing a song such as "Twinkle, Twinkle, Little Star" as they scrub their hands with soap and water, to make sure they are not just rushing through the process.

**2** Have your children get in the habit of washing their hands whenever they get ready to leave the bathroom. This means after sitting on the toilet (whether they went or not) and even after a diaper change. Post picture signs by the sink, reminding them of the steps.

**3** When you are using a changing table, use careful sanitary techniques. Check with your local board of health or licensing agency for the proper procedures for your area. Most health departments also have posters reminding you of the steps.

**4** Keep spray bottles filled with a bleach and water solution for disinfecting. Mix 2 tablespoons bleach with 1 gallon water. Label bottles with contents.

**5** After flushing toilets, spray them with a disinfectant. To clean a potty chair after use, disinfect it with a bleach and water solution before it is used again.

**8** After your children are up from their naps, disinfect the cots or mats with a bleach and water solution. Stack and store them until the next day's use.

**9** Use care when wiping your children's noses. Use disposable tissues, put them in the wastebasket immediately, and wash your hands right away.

**10** To protect your hands from being chapped from frequent hand washing, try using a lotion soap or an extra-strength hand lotion.

**6** Disinfect and wash your toys on a regular basis, at least once a week. Put them through a dishwasher or follow this washing-by-hand procedure. Set out three containers of water. Fill the first one with warm soapy water to clean the toys. Fill the second one with clean water to rinse the toys. Fill the final tub with a bleach and water solution to disinfect and sanitize the toys. Allow the toys to air dry.

**7** Have a container set aside for toys that your children have put in their mouths. If you notice a toddler putting a toy in his or her mouth, wait until he or she is done and then put the toy in the container. As time permits, disinfect the mouthed toys using the method stated in tip 6.

# Successful Eating Times

**1** Encourage your toddlers to serve themselves whenever they can. You will have to serve some types of foods, of course, but give the children the opportunity to serve themselves easy-to-handle foods such as bread, crackers, and fruit slices.

**2** Put only a little food on a toddler's plate. It is much easier to give seconds than it is to clean up food from the table or floor. Fill glasses only half full, then refill when necessary. A good rule of thumb is to give a child only as much food or drink as you are willing to clean up.

**3** Select some soft background music to play while your children eat. The music helps to set the mood and keep everyone relaxed.

**4** When it is time to eat, make sure that all is ready (food, plates, utensils, napkins, glasses, etc.) before asking your toddlers to wash up and come to the table.

**5** Have everyone in the room sit down and eat at the same time. This includes all adults. Ask the adults to space themselves among the children to offer help and to model appropriate table manners.

**6** Toddlers still need to wear bibs to protect their clothing. Disposable bibs are very handy to use and make cleanup easy.

**7** Select utensils, plates, and glasses that are easy for your toddlers to use. Glasses should be small enough for your children to hold with one hand. Spoons should be short enough to get to their mouths easily.

**8** Encourage as much self-feeding as possible. Toddlers need lots of practice. Yes, there will be messes, but the growth in self-help skills and self-confidence is worth it.

**9** Plan what you will do when lunch is over. Where will extra food go? Where will dirty dishes go? How will the toddlers help? This eliminates confusion and makes the transition to the next activity, usually a quiet one before naptime, less hectic.

**10** Let your toddlers help wash the table and chairs with cloths while you sweep up the floor. This cooperative effort keeps everyone happy and busy.

# Potty Training

**1** Potty training is an important milestone for toddlers. The process of learning to recognize when they have to go, getting to the bathroom on time, unfastening clothes, wiping, refastening clothes, flushing, and washing hands is quite long. This is not a simple process. And it takes a lot of patience on the part of everyone involved—parents, teachers, and, most importantly, toddlers.

**2** Educate your children's parents about potty training. Explain to them that there is a window of opportunity for potty training a toddler. Teach them about the signs that their children are ready to use the toilet: an awareness of what is happening, the ability to communicate, and the motivation to be out of diapers.

**3** Discuss your potty training techniques with each toddler's parents and ask for their input. Try to reach an agreement on how you will approach potty training with each child so there can be a consistent message between day care and home.

**4** Try to have the diaper changing facilities and the toddlers' toilets in the same bathroom, close to the toddler room. It makes it easier for you because some children are wearing diapers, some are potty trained, and still more are in-between. It is also easier for your children because they begin to associate one room for bathrooming.

**5** It is best to have child-size toilets and sinks in the bathroom. If this is not possible, be sure to have slip-proof stools available.

**6** Try to have your children use toilets instead of potty chairs. Potty chairs are germ collectors, hard to keep sanitary, and too easy to spill when full. And, for some children, the transition from potty chair to toilet can be difficult, and it is just easier to start on the toilet.

**7** Have your children stay in diapers or diapered underpants until potty training has progressed to the point of just a few accidents. The more accidents there are in the toddler room, the more difficult it is to keep sanitary.

**8** To introduce your toddlers to the potty, have them sit down on the toilet for a very short period of time. This is just to get used to the idea of sitting there. Repeat this every so often, and at some point, they will actually go.

**9** Praise your toddlers when they do use the toilet and be sure not to criticize any accidents. Using the toilet is a skill that takes most toddlers several months to figure out.

**10** You may want to keep records about when each child has a diaper change or uses the toilet. This helps you see progress, and it is important information for parents.

# Word Play

# Encouraging Language

**1** Have conversations with your toddlers at every opportunity. Describe what you are doing and encourage them to talk about what they are doing. Take advantage of one-on-one times you have with each child, such as settling down for a nap, changing a diaper, or just sitting together.

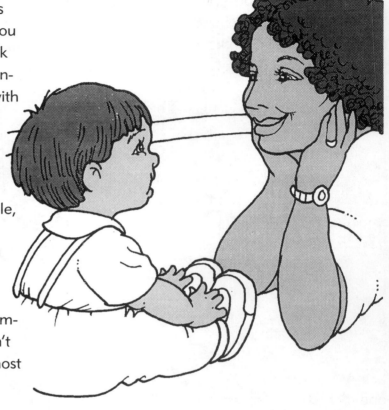

**2** Help your children fill in the gaps when they speak to you. For example, if a child says, "Blocks down," help him or her expand that to "Yes, you knocked the blocks down."

**3** When your toddlers are trying to communicate with you and you just don't understand, ask questions. While most toddlers are using more than one-word sentences, some may still just use one word when they want something or when they are tired. If a toddler says, "Na, na," and you are not sure what that means, ask, "Do you want your blanket? Do you want a banana?" In addition to finding out what the child needs, you are also modeling language for him or her.

**4** Toddlers often gesture or point to items they want or need. While you should continue to support this form of communication, it is important to give toddlers the words they need and encourage them to use them.

**5** Most toddlers mispronounce words. Avoid criticizing or even correcting your children when they do this. If a child is constantly corrected, he or she will eventually give up trying. When a child does pronounce a word incorrectly, respond by using that word pronounced correctly. For example, if the child says, "I want the redsy one," you can reply, "Here is the red car."

**6** Toddlers talk to themselves a great deal, especially as they are playing. Encourage this self-expression as much as possible. You may even want to get them started by sitting with them and saying, "Zoom, zoom," as you push a toy car along the floor.

**7** Young children need to hear and learn words that tell what they see (*street, car, doll*), words that tell what they do (*run, walk, play*), words that tell how things look and feel (*soft, cold, big, small*), and words that tell how they feel (*sad, mad, happy, afraid*).

**8** Be a good language model for your toddlers. Talk to them in complete sentences, being sure to use good pronunciation and grammar. Face your children, make eye contact, and try not to use or encourage baby talk.

**9** Try not to ask your children too many questions at one time and be careful about overloading your conversations with too much information. Use simple, short sentences and encourage conversation by repeating what they say.

**10** After asking one of your children a question, be sure to give him or her enough time to answer it before you jump in. Young children need time to organize their thoughts and find the right words. An easy way to do this is to count slowly (and silently) to ten after asking a question to allow time for the toddler to begin speaking.

# Language Through Music

**1** Children and music go together. Toddlers love singing, which encourages verbal skills. They can usually learn parts of songs or single words of songs. It is best to just use your voice and not other instruments when singing with toddlers, so they can really hear the words.

**2** Select a few songs that are simple and have motions to act out, such as "Eensy, Weensy Spider," "I'm a Little Teapot," or "Rock-a-Bye Baby." Keep the number of songs sung in the toddler room to a minimum, because toddlers need and love repetition. They want to hear and sing the same few songs over and over again. This is a good way for them to learn and practice their language skills.

**3** Take the time to really learn the songs you are singing with your toddlers. Practice them, if needed, and know all the words and motions. This way, you are not distracted while you are singing with the children, and you can give them your full attention.

**4** When you sing with your toddlers, sit on the floor and encourage them to sit and sing with you. Smile and enjoy yourself. Don't worry if your singing voice is not perfect; they don't care. They just want to enjoy the music with you.

**5** Try singing an "open-ended" song in which your children fill in the blank. For example, a very simple song would be "Here we go round the _____." Your children will love filling in and singing their own words.

**6** Make up a simple song about whatever your children are doing. Just a line or two, such as "The children are playing with blocks today; they're having lots of fun," repeated in a singsong voice or sung to a favorite melody, is sure to interest your children.

**7** When you sing with your toddlers, encourage them to clap along. This gives them a sense of the rhythm of the music and words. Clapping also works with rhymes.

**8** Let your children dance and move around while they listen to favorite songs. Getting all parts of their bodies involved in the language experience makes it more fun and interesting.

**9** Use soft music at naptime to quiet your children. Select lullaby tapes with gentle, soothing words.

**10** Sing songs with children's names in them. This is a great way to get a single child's attention. It also reinforces name recognition among other children.

# Successful Storytimes

**1** Good storytimes are quiet, warm, and intimate. Frustrating storytimes are hectic and forced. Schedule storytime when you know you will not be rushed or busy and when your children will be able to focus their attention. For example, after lunch is a better time for stories than just before your children eat.

**2** Sit on the floor with your children during storytime and hold the book so everyone can see. Practice reading the book ahead of time so you are familiar with the words and can emphasize important parts.

**3** Don't expect all of your children to come to storytime, and expect some children to leave the group when their attention span runs out. Sit where you can see the entire room and communicate the story to all of the children, even the ones who are not sitting with you.

**4** Have story mats available for your children who would like to sit and listen to your story. These mats could be carpet samples, small towels, or felt squares. Arrange the mats so that each child has his or her own space. Ask the children to sit on the mats while they are listening to the story.

**5** Choose books for storytime that are short, have large pictures that are easily seen, and have a simple story line instead of just pictures to identify. Select story lines about things toddlers can relate to. Topics such as food, clothing, or bedtime are examples.

**6** When you read a book, use your voice and let the story come alive. Read slowly and be dramatic. Keep eye contact with the children. Think about reading *to* them and not *at* them.

**7** Read stories your children like hearing. Toddlers love stories with repetition. They also love to hear the same stories day after day. If you find your children do not enjoy a particular book, they may not be ready for it yet.

**8** Tell stories that have lots of sound effects. Your children can use their hands or feet to add the sounds of a galloping horse, beating drums, a rainstorm, or a ball bouncing.

**9** One way to extend your children's interest in storytime is to use story props. One or two puppets or a few flannelboard characters can make a story come alive. If you do use props, it works best to select just one kind, puppets or flannelboard characters, for example. Using both is too difficult for the children to follow.

**10** Tell this story that your children will want to hear over and over again. Collect a few props and put them in a box. Take the props out of the box one at a time and use them to tell a story about your children. Be sure to include each child in at least one part of the story.

# Puppets

**1** Young children are naturally curious about puppets, and puppets are a great way to encourage language. Some children may even prefer talking to puppets over talking to people. Hand puppets or finger puppets work equally well. It is important to have well-constructed ones. Soft puppets work best with young children.

**2** A hand puppet can tell a story or introduce storytime to your children. If you use a puppet to announce storytime every day, it will become an automatic signal to your children and they will know what to expect whenever they see it. Let your puppet develop his or her own "personality."

**3** Young children need some instructions on how to treat puppets. Teach them not to put their hands in the puppets' mouth and to not hit the puppets. Children who are not familiar with puppets often react in this way when they are excited or overstimulated.

**4** When you use puppets to represent the characters of a story, have the puppets act out the story without too much narration. When you read from a book and use a puppet, your children become distracted and confused because they are not sure which one to follow.

**5** Sock puppets are simplest to make. Pull the end of the sock inside the hand to form the mouth. Draw on eyes and lips with permanent markers. Glue on a red felt "tongue," if you wish.

**8** Sometimes it's handy to have a two-faced puppet. For example, if you are telling a story about a child who is happy and sad, one side could be a happy face and the other side could be a sad face. To make the puppet, staple two paper plates together, front to front, with a craft stick taped in between. Then draw a face on each side of the puppet.

**9** To make a set of finger puppets, cut the fingertips off an old glove. Use felt tip markers to draw facial features on each fingertip. Put two or more of the finger puppets on your fingers and let them talk to your children or tell a story.

**10** Sticker puppets are probably the easiest finger puppets of all. Just place a different sticker on each finger and let the sticker characters do the talking.

**6** Toddlers love pop-up puppets. To make one, insert a straw into a small plastic foam ball. With felt tip markers, add facial features, and glue on yarn hair, if you wish. Poke a hole in the bottom of a paper cup and push the straw through the hole. Move the straw up and down to make the puppet pop up.

**7** A nose puppet is fun to make. Turn a paper cup upside down and cut a small circle out of the side. This is the nose hole. Draw the rest of the facial features around the nose hole, and add yarn hair. Put your index finger through the hole for the nose, and then make the puppet "talk."

# Flannelboard Fun

**1** Toddlers love flannelboard stories. For best results, select stories that are simple and need just a few flannelboard pieces.

**2** When presenting a flannelboard story, try to *tell* it in your own words to your children, rather than *reading* it to them. You will be amazed at how quickly you lose their attention if you are struggling with the words to the story and where to put which flannelboard piece.

**3** A carpet sample works well for an easy and inexpensive flannelboard. Many carpet stores will sell or give away their old carpet samples. You could have two or three squares of varying sizes to use with different numbers of flannelboard pieces.

**4** You can also make a flannelboard out of an old fold-up gameboard by gluing felt to the front of it. (If you wish, arrange the felt on the gameboard to create a simple scene, such as a garden or a room.) Set the gameboard on its edge and bend the sides in a little to make it stand up.

**5** You can create an instant flannelboard area by attaching, at your children's eye level, a large square of flannel or felt to the back of a bookcase or a room divider.

**6** Make characters for your flannelboard by cutting character shapes out of felt pieces. Add details, such as facial features or clothing, by cutting pieces out of felt scraps and gluing them on, or by simply drawing them on with permanent markers.

**7** You can cut characters out of magazines or old storybooks. Trim the pictures and mount them on heavy paper, if necessary, then glue strips of felt or flannel to the backs of the pictures.

**8** Thick spongy paper towels work well for flannelboard pieces. Simply cut the shapes out of the towels and decorate them with felt tip markers.

**9** Store flannelboard pieces for each story in a separate envelope. You can also write the story or rhyme on the front of the envelope to help you remember the details of the story.

**10** If you have a permanent flannelboard area, leave several flannelboard characters and pieces available for your toddlers to play with. They will love putting the pieces on the board and taking them off again. They may even make up a short story.

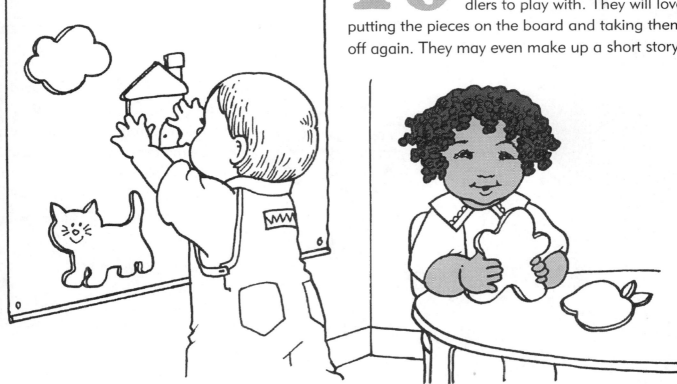

# Exploring Opposites

**1** Your toddlers will love this sensory experience. Collect several feather dusters, cut the feathers off, and place them in a box. Let your toddlers take off their shoes and socks and walk barefoot in the feathers. Then, have them walk on a hard floor. Talk about how soft the feathers feel and how hard the floor feels.

**2** Play the Elevator Game to teach your children the difference between up and down. Have them pretend to go up in an elevator, raising their bodies up and up until they are on tiptoe. Next have them pretend to go down in the elevator, lowering their bodies to the floor. Repeat as often as your children like.

**3** Clapping can teach your children about fast and slow. Clap your hands quickly and ask your children to clap along with you. Next, clap your hands very slowly and have them try to do the same.

**4** Singing is a great way to teach your children about loud and quiet. Ask them to sing a favorite song, such as "Row, Row, Row Your Boat," as loudly as they can, and then sing it as quietly as they can.

**5** Push and pull toys are great for helping toddlers experience opposites. Whenever you see children playing with the push and pull toys, talk with them about what they are doing. "Kara, you are pulling that wagon. Bart, I see you are pushing the stroller."

**9** Talk about in and out as your toddlers play the following game. Set out a container and some blocks. Sit with your toddlers as they put the blocks in the container and then take them out. Say the words "in" and "out" as the toddlers are performing the actions.

**10** The concepts of off and on are fun to explore with a light switch. Invite your children to sit on the floor by a light switch. Place a step stool next to your light switch and select the first child to turn the lights off and then on. As the lights go off, have everyone say "Off," and as they go on, have everyone say "On." Let each child have a chance to turn the lights off and on.

**6** Show your toddlers the difference be tween long and short with this activity. Cut a piece of adding machine tape to the same height as one of your children, and tape it to the wall. Now cut a piece of adding machine tape to the same height as a teddy bear in your room, and tape it next to the child's. Have the child notice how long his or her tape is and how short teddy's is. Repeat for each child.

**7** Teach hot and cold with a bowl of ice cubes and a bowl of warm water. Your toddlers will love experiencing the differences between the temperatures in the two bowls.

**8** Introduce your children to rough and smooth textures with this fun experi- ence. Set out a piece of cardboard with rough sandpaper glued to one side and aluminum foil glued to the other. Let the children feel the difference.

# Words Everywhere

**1** Creating a print-rich environment is fun and important for toddlers. It introduces them to language, letters, and words. As they get older, they will begin to see that the lines on the signs are letters, the letters make words, and the words have meaning. This is the foundation for reading, vocabulary, and other important language skills.

**2** Make your environment print-rich by labeling as many things as possible. For instance, write the word "door" on a piece of paper and tape it to the door at your children's eye level; write "blocks" and tape it by the blocks; and so on. Use large, written words on bulletin boards. Display a calendar for each month. It is important for your children to get used to seeing lots of words and written language in their environment.

**3** Attach your children's names to the areas that contain their clothes and their artwork, and any other separate areas they have.

**4** Look for pictures and posters with words on them. Talk to your children about what the words say. You can make the pictures touchable by laminating them, covering them with clear self-stick paper, or mounting them in acrylic plastic frames. This way, toddlers can look and touch as they explore the pictures. Talk with the toddlers about what they see in the pictures.

**5** Print out the rules of your group and add simple picture symbols. Post the rules at your children's eye level.

**6** Draw several feeling faces, or faces that express different emotions. Label each face with its feeling name. Hang the faces on a wall or a bulletin board. Help your children name the feelings pictured.

**7** Make placemats for your children with their names on them. Let them use the placemats at snack and lunchtime.

**8** Tape a sheet of paper to a cupboard. Whenever your children notice something that is needed for the classroom, let them watch as you write down the item on your list. Set out paper and chubby crayons for them to "write" their own lists.

**9** Use large magnets with words on them to hold notes and other papers to magnetic surfaces.

**10** Look for an area carpet with letters or numbers on it and place it in your large muscle skills area. Let your children hop from letter to letter or from number to number. Talk about the numbers and letters on the carpet.

# Language Games

**4** Play "What do I do?" with your children. Hold up an object for them to look at. If you wish, let them each have a turn holding the object. Then ask the children to tell you what it does.

**5** Give your children simple directions to follow, such as "Touch your nose. Clap your hands. Sit on the floor." If you like, let them say directions for you to follow.

**1** Toddlers love this word game. Collect a variety of familiar items and put them in a box. Let them pull the items out one at a time as you help them name the items.

**2** You can play a variation of the game above by finding photographs (not illustrations) of familiar things. Glue the photos to heavy paper and cover them with clear self-stick paper. Show each picture to a small group of toddlers and encourage them to name it.

**3** Name body parts with your children. You can make a game out of it by asking them to touch their nose, an arm, a leg, a foot, etc.

**9** Ask your children to think of what's needed for certain events. For example, "What do we need to wear to keep our hands warm outside? What do we need to pour milk into so we can drink it?"

**10** Help your children learn one another's names with this game. Have the children sit in a circle with their legs spread out and their feet touching. Roll a ball to the first child and say, "Catch the ball, Dominick. Now roll it over to Ella." Repeat until each child has had a chance to catch and roll the ball at least once.

**6** Help your children learn to correctly pronounce the beginning and ending sounds of words by playing this game. Have the children look around the room and find certain objects that you name. Stress the beginning and ending sounds of the names as you say them. Try to use one-syllable words such as hat, boat, car, or book.

**7** Make a sound like a train and invite your toddlers to make the sound along with you. Make other sounds for them to imitate. Help them name the sounds as well. If you put actions with the sounds, the children will imitate the sounds more quickly and easily.

**8** Look for opportunities to count with your children. Count as you go up stairs. Count as you fasten snaps on coats. Count out crackers at snacktime. This is a great way to introduce numbers and rote counting to your toddlers.

# Language Props

**1** A language prop is simply an object that helps encourage your children's language development. Almost anything can become a language prop.

A wonderful prop that encourages language and observation skills is a fish tank. Set up the tank where you and your children can watch the fish together. Talk about the colors of the fish, what they are doing, what you are doing as you take care of them, and so on.

**2** A toy telephone is a natural language prop. Have a child pretend to "call" you on the phone. You can have very interesting conversations over the "phone."

**3** Set up a microphone in your room. A microphone can be added to most stereo systems, and many children's tape recorders have microphones on them. Let your children take turns talking into the microphone. Soft-spoken children especially benefit from this language prop because everyone can hear them much more clearly.

**4** Tape record your children's voices. Let them take turns talking or singing into the microphone while you record them. Play back their voices for them to listen to. They love talking just to hear their voices on the tape.

**5** Set up a dollhouse with toddler-safe pieces. Let your children set up the dollhouse however they wish, making the various people talk to one another. This language prop offers children the opportunity to expand their "social" vocabulary—the words they need for interacting with others.

**6** Give each of your children a scarf. Ask the children to move their scarves in various ways, such as up, down, and around in a circle. You can also ask them to put their scarves on their heads, under a chair, over their knees, and so on.

**7** Set up a mirror on a table or, better yet, hang a full-length mirror in your classroom. Look in the mirror with one of your children. Ask your child to make a happy face with you. Look at both of your reflections. Make other faces with your child, such as angry, sad, tired, and excited.

**8** Set out several boxes for your children to explore. As they imagine the boxes are baby cradles, trains, cars, or basketball hoops, help them find the words to describe what they are doing.

**9** Put several jingle bells in a plastic jar. Put glue around the rim and screw the lid on tightly. Make a jar for each of your children. Let them shake their bell jars for a while. Then have them hold their jars still while you tell a story about bells. Ask your children to listen carefully to the story, and every time they hear the word "bells," have them shake their jingle jars.

**10** A box of dress-up clothes makes a wonderful language prop. Let your children try on the clothes. Talk about the various clothes. Help them describe how the clothes are being put on—over their heads, putting their arms in, pulling the pants up, etc. Talk about the colors of their clothes. Describe what the children look like when they are all dressed up—handsome, pretty, funny, scary.

# Discovery Play

# Water Fun

**1** Water is an integral part of the toddler classroom. It is both soothing and exciting, and a wonderful activity for distracting children as they learn to separate from their parents.

**2** If you use a commercial water table, be sure it has a good drain. The table should be low enough for a toddler to stand and play in the water without the water running down his or her arms.

**3** If you opt for individual containers for water (dishpans and small plastic bathtubs work well), place them on a very low table or even on a shower curtain or a large beach towel on the floor.

**4** Before they start playing in a tub of water, have your children wash their hands. This helps to keep the water clean. Be sure to change the water and sanitize the container and all the water toys each day.

**5** Closely supervise your children as they play in the water. You can model appropriate behavior, helping to remind your toddlers that the water should stay in the tub. Also make sure your toddlers understand that they cannot drink the water in the water table.

**6** Give your children waterproof paint smocks to wear before they play in the water. Help them put on the smocks and roll up their sleeves to keep their clothes as dry as possible.

**7** Be sure to have towels and a mop handy for cleaning up any spills. Even young children can learn to help you wipe up any water that accidentally splashes out.

**8** Varying the temperature of the water in the water table changes the experience for young children. The water can be toasty warm one day, room temperature the next.

**9** Be sure to include a variety of equipment for exploring water. Your children will love experimenting with cups, small plastic containers, toy boats, small plastic pitchers, and so on.

**10** Occasionally, add a small amount of dishwashing detergent for bubbles or a few drops of food coloring to change the color of the water. Your children will love the new experience.

# Sand Play

**1** Toddlers love to play in sand. When children are outside, they will play in sand if it is available, or if it is not, they will play in the dirt or gravel. It is preferable to have a sandbox with clean sand.

**2** Toddlers want to climb into the sandbox and sit while they play. Be sure the sandbox or sand area is large enough for them to do this. They need a lot of space for effective sand play.

**3** Stay with your children during sand play, whether it is at a sandbox outside or a sand table indoors. Model appropriate sand play and make sure that sand stays in the box or the table and is not eaten or thrown.

**4** Sandbox toys can include shovels, scoops, pails, cups, dishes, muffin tins, pots, pie pans, plastic containers, and toy trucks. Make sure that metal toys are replaced often or are rust-proof. Also check occasionally for sharp edges. Be sure you have enough toys for your children to play comfortably without having to share.

**5** If you have a sandbox outside, be sure it has a cover to keep it protected from animals when it is not in use.

**6** The outdoor sand area should be in a place where shade is available to keep the sand cool and to protect your children from the sun. You can position a beach umbrella, set up a canopy, or hang up a blanket to create the necessary protection.

**7** Toddlers love playing with wet sand. When the weather is warm, carry a few buckets of water to the sand area. Let your children make handprints in the wet sand. Have them take off their shoes and feel the cool, wet sand with their bare feet.

**8** Sand play is also possible indoors. You can use a commercially made sand table or you can make individual sandboxes out of plastic dishpans or cardboard boxes. Be sure the table is low enough for your children to play there comfortably. Set individual sandboxes on the floor. You can also set up a child's wading pool indoors and fill it with sand. Your children will want to sit in it as they do outdoors. Be sure to keep a small broom and a dustpan close by for easy cleanup.

**9** Indoor sand containers can be filled with materials other than sand. You can use split peas, dried corn, or rice. Be sure to closely supervise your children while they are playing to make sure they keep the materials in the containers and to prevent the children from eating them.

**10** Remember that sand play can be messy. Sand will get into children's clothes and shoes. Help them dump sand out of their shoes and brush it off their clothes. Remind the children's parents that sand play is important and worth the little bit of mess it might cause.

# Modeling Dough Fun

**1** For toddlers, the fun of playing with modeling dough is making *changes*, not *things*. Encourage them to find ways to roll, pound, flatten, and squish the dough.

**2** Remember that toddlers do not have a lot of strength in their fingers and hands yet. Soft dough is easiest for them to play with. If you are using commercially made dough, be sure to knead it well before you give it to your children.

**3** For a no-mess activity, put lumps of soft modeling dough in resealable plastic bags and let your children pound and squish the bags of dough.

**4** Even young toddlers can help you make a simple modeling dough. Just combine 1 cup flour, 1/4 cup salt, 1/3 cup water, and a few drops of food coloring in a bowl. Mix well and play.

**5** Cloud Dough is a soft, easily manipulated dough that is perfect for little fingers. Mix together 3 cups flour, 3/4 cup vegetable oil, 1/2 cup water, and a few drops of food coloring in a bowl. Knead well until the dough is soft and elastic (add more water if necessary). This dough is somewhat oily, so it is best played with on a washable surface.

**6** Make one of the dough recipes on the opposite page, except do not add the food coloring with the rest of the ingredients. Roll the dough into several balls. Put a drop or two of food coloring in the middle of each ball. Give the dough balls to your children to pound and squish and let them discover the color inside.

**7** When making your own modeling dough, try heating up the water before mixing the ingredients together. Let your children play with the warm dough for a different sensory experience.

**8** Craft sticks are a wonderful tool for your children to use while they are playing with modeling dough. Craft sticks can be pushed into the dough, used to "cut" off little pieces, and used to poke holes in the dough.

**9** When your children are playing with modeling dough, be sure to have several sizes and kinds of containers for them. Toddlers love to fill containers with dough and then take it out again. Suggestions include empty yogurt containers, a muffin tin, a small cake pan, or metal lids.

**10** For a change of pace, give each of your children a small piece of bread dough (frozen bread dough, available at grocery stores, works well after it has thawed for a few hours). Let your children mold their pieces into whatever shapes they would like. Bake their creations according to the package or recipe directions. Serve the children their bread shapes for snack.

# Exploring With Crayons

**1** Even young toddlers enjoy using crayons. Large crayons are easier for little fingers to hold and learn to control. If you take the paper off the crayons, your children will have another way to use them.

**2** Encourage your children's beginning attempts at using crayons. Remember that their drawings reflect the early stages of drawing—primarily random scribblings with a few shapes. This is a time for them to explore what to *do* with a crayon, not what to *draw* with it.

**3** Limit the number of crayons you make available to each child. Two or three are enough. Be sure to give each child his or her own crayons. A tub of crayons for everyone to share does not work well with this age group.

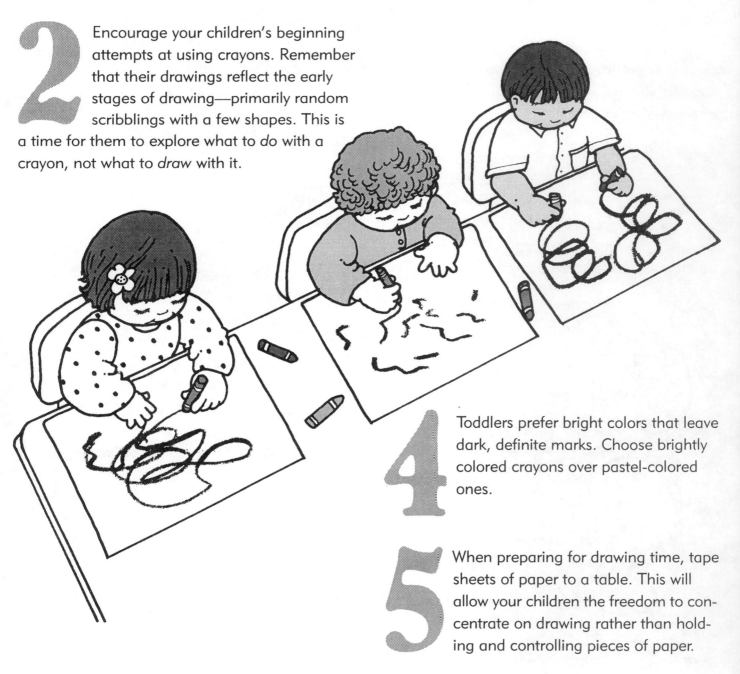

**4** Toddlers prefer bright colors that leave dark, definite marks. Choose brightly colored crayons over pastel-colored ones.

**5** When preparing for drawing time, tape sheets of paper to a table. This will allow your children the freedom to concentrate on drawing rather than holding and controlling pieces of paper.

**6** If you prefer, cover the entire table with butcher paper, newsprint, or other large sheets of paper for a no-slip drawing surface.

**7** Be sure to take the time to sit at the table with your children while they are drawing. Model the types of drawings your children are capable of—scribbles, lines, and other simple marks.

**8** Play this drawing game with one of your children. Ask the child to make a mark, then you make the same mark next to his or hers. Let the child continue making marks for you to copy.

**9** For a different drawing experience, tape pairs of unwrapped crayons together. Let your children experiment making marks with these new crayon pairs.

**10** Instead of drawing on paper, try this: Collect several cardboard boxes that are big enough for your children to sit in. Have them climb into the boxes and give them each one or two crayons to use to decorate the insides.

# Time to Paint

**1** Fingerpainting is one of the most basic painting experiences for young children. The easiest way to introduce this activity is to put the fingerpaint directly on a washable table. Let your children sit at the table and paint. Some children put their whole hands in and paint away. Others are more cautious and begin by just watching or by putting in a finger or two. Allow your children to experiment as they need.

**2** If you decide to use paintbrushes with your toddlers, select ones that have a large brush area and a short handle. The easel-type paintbrush works well.

**3** Paint shirts are a must for protecting your children's clothing. Plastic aprons in the appropriate size for toddlers work best.

**4** If you are having your children paint on paper, remember that you can use almost any kind, such as computer paper, grocery bags, cardboard, butcher paper, and construction paper. Sheets of newspaper taped to a table also work well.

**5** In addition to painting with paintbrushes, you can let your toddlers explore painting with craft sticks, large feathers, or sponges.

**6** When setting out paint, put it in wide, shallow containers that are hard to tip over. You may want to invest in special paint cups with lids that minimize spilling, or make your own out of plastic containers with lids.

**7** In addition to painting at a table, toddlers can paint at an easel. Make sure the easel is at a height that allows your children to stand and paint. Use a drop cloth under the easel to collect spills. Easel painting especially requires the direct supervision of a teacher.

**8** You may want to consider using "edible" paints for your toddlers. Pudding, yogurt, whipped cream, and gelatin that has not completely set are possibilities. When using paint of this sort, have your children wash their hands first. For each child, place a small amount of the "paint" on a baking sheet or a clean table. Let the children fingerpaint as they wish.

**9** Tape a large sheet of paper to a wall or a fence outside. Fill spray bottles with a lot of water and a little tempera paint. Let your toddlers spray-paint the paper with the colored water.

**10** Hang a mirror on a wall or securely prop one up on a table, and set out tempera paint and a paintbrush. Invite one of your children to sit in front of the mirror and paint on it as he or she wishes. Use a damp cloth to clean the mirror for the next child.

# Creative Art Fun

**1** Set out paper baking cups, shallow containers of glue, and construction paper. Show your toddlers how to dip the baking cups in the glue and then put them on the construction paper. Let them glue the cups on the paper however they wish.

**2** Toddlers love to tear paper. This activity provides them with an acceptable way of doing just that. Set out as many different kinds of lightweight paper as you can. Let your children tear the paper into small pieces. Help them glue the pieces onto a large sheet of paper to make a torn-paper collage.

**3** Your toddlers will love the colorful results of this activity. Cut clear self-stick paper into large squares. Remove the backing and tape the squares to a table, sticky side up. Cut various colors of cellophane paper into small squares. Let your children arrange the squares on their sticky papers. When they are finished, hang the colorful squares in a window where the children can see them.

**4** Set out simple rubber stamps and washable ink pads. Cover a table with butcher paper and let your children "stamp away." Show them how to press a rubber stamp on an ink pad and then onto the paper to make a print. Encourage them to experiment with making as many prints as they would like.

**5** To make a fluffy cloud for your wall, cut white or clear self-stick paper into a cloud shape. Remove the backing and tape the shape to the wall, sticky side out, at the children's level. Set out a pile of jumbo-size cotton balls. Let your children place the cotton balls on the cloud shape until it is completely covered. Encourage them to feel the soft cloud they just made.

**6** Pour a thin layer of white paint into a shallow container. Show your children how to dip their thumbs into the paint and then onto dark blue paper to make snowflake prints.

**7** Young children love exploring stickers. They enjoy sticking them on themselves as much as they do sticking them on paper. The easiest stickers for toddlers to use are the small sheets of circle stickers found where office supplies are sold. They come in bright colors and are very easy to remove from the page. To make other stickers easier for young children to use, remove them from their sticker page and place them on a sheet of waxed paper.

**8** Paper-plate crowns are fun and easy for toddlers to make. Give each of your children a paper plate to decorate with crayons. When they are finished, fold and cut the plates as shown in the illustration to make crowns.

**9** Let your toddlers create with shapes you have cut out of felt. Have them arrange the shapes on a flannelboard or a carpet square.

**10** Color a piece of butcher paper with pencils or pastels. Tape the paper to a table. Give your children large art gum erasers and let them erase the color from the paper.

# Discovering the Senses

**1** Introduce your children to the five senses with a food such as an orange or a banana. Give each child a piece of the fruit. Talk about the way it looks, smells, feels, sounds, and tastes.

**2** Your children will love playing this sight game. Place a stuffed animal in a basket and cover it with a small blanket. Let your children lift up the blanket and peek into the basket to see what they can find.

**3** Toddlers love surprises. Encourage them to use their sense of sight to find this surprise. Each day, bring a new item in, such as a box, a laundry basket, or a beanbag chair. Let your children look around each day as they arrive to discover the new item.

**4** Make a touch-and-tell box. Cut several holes in a shoebox and place two or three familiar items inside of it. Have one of your children put his or her hand in the box and touch the items inside. Can he or she guess what they are? For younger toddlers, let them watch you put items in the box and give them verbal cues. "I have put a spoon, a toy kitty, and a doll bottle in the box. Would you like to feel what's in the box?"

**5** Make small pillows out of different textures of fabric. For example, you could make pillows out of nylon, cotton, corduroy, fake fur, flannel, and denim. Have your children feel the different texture of each pillow. Help them describe each one.

**6** Find a large appliance box and set it up. Cover the inside and outside walls of the box with materials of various textures, such as foil, sandpaper, sponges, textured wallpaper, fake fur, and corrugated cardboard. Let your children explore the walls of the box. Encourage them to describe the different textures to you.

**7** Play this listening game with your children. Turn on some music and have your children dance along. Tell them that when they hear the music stop, they need to stop their dancing, and when they hear the music start they can start dancing again.

**8** Make smelling cups for your toddlers to explore. Collect several empty yogurt containers and lids. Put a few cotton balls in each container. Drop a different liquid scent into each container, such as vanilla extract, lemon flavoring, and perfume. Put the lids on the containers and poke a few holes in the top of each lid. Let your children sniff the different cups and tell you which one is their favorite.

**9** Your children will love crawling on this textured floor. Cut the lids off egg cartons and save them for another activity. Tape the cup sides of the egg cartons to a small area of a tiled floor. Let the children take their shoes off and walk or crawl across the bumpy surface.

**10** Cut an opening in a sturdy paper plate and tape colored cellophane over it. Make one of these plates for each of your children. Let your children look through the opening in their plate. What does the room look like? What do you look like?

# Science Exploration

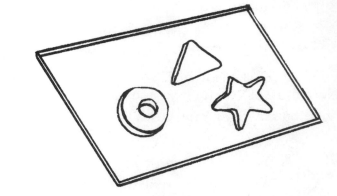

**3** Magnets are a favorite with young children. Put out several nonaluminum baking sheets and large magnets. (Make sure the magnets are too large for your children to swallow or choke on.) Let your children play with the magnets, taking them off the baking sheets and putting them back on. Can they find any other places where the magnets will stick?

**1** Young children learn best when they can see and touch whatever they are learning about. Have a science table in your room with safe objects that your children can manipulate and experiment with. Following are suggestions for items to have or make for your science table.

**4** Attach a full-length mirror to a wall by the science table. Make sure the mirror goes all the way down to the floor. Encourage your children to look into the mirror. What do they see? Can they make the image in the mirror move around? Can they make it crouch down, jump up, turn around, or stand on tiptoe?

**2** Collect two clear-plastic 2-liter bottles. Fill each bottle halfway with water. Into one bottle, place small items that will sink, such as a bolt, a penny, and a marble. Into the other bottle, place small items that will float, such as a feather, a crumpled foil ball, and a plastic toy. Put glue around the rims and tightly screw on the lids. Let your children experiment with the bottles, turning them this way and that to see what the objects do.

**5** Young children love exploring with this unique wave bottle. Fill a clear-plastic jar two-thirds full with water and add several drops of blue food coloring. Fill the jar to the rim with mineral oil, getting rid of as many bubbles as possible. Put glue around the rim of the jar and tightly screw on the lid. Let your children hold the jar sideways and gently tip it to create waves.

**6** Set out an infant scale and let your children use it to weigh dolls and stuffed animals.

**7** Make this simple sorter for your children to use. Cut one large hole and one small hole in the lid of a shoebox. Put the lid on the box. Set out large and small items and let your children sort them by putting the small items into the box through the small hole and the large items into the box through the large hole.

**8** Find an unbreakable sand timer to set out on the science table. Your children will love watching the sand flow from top to bottom.

**9** Place a scoop of sand into a clear plastic jar. Fill the jar with water, put glue around the rim, and screw the lid on tightly. Have your children shake the jar to mix up the sand and water and then set it on a table. Let them watch as the sand slowly sinks to the bottom of the jar. You could also find one of those plastic snow scene jars for your children to shake and watch.

**10** Collect three clear-plastic jars with lids (peanut butter jars work well). Place nuts and bolts in one jar, dried beans in another, and salt in a third. Put glue around the rims of the jars and screw on the lids. Let your children shake the jars. Ask them which one is the loudest and which one is the quietest. If you wish, let them think of other kinds of materials you could use to make more "noise jars."

# Encouraging Curiosity

**1** Tape butcher paper over a large portion of the floor. Let your children stand, crawl, and sit on the newly covered floor. The next day, cut a circle in the middle of the paper and let your children explore. On each subsequent day, remove more of the paper, giving the children a different perception of the floor covering each time. Continue until all the paper is removed.

**2** Collect several paper grocery bags. Cut a hole in the bottom of each bag and several smaller holes on the sides. Set the bags upright on the floor. Encourage your toddlers to play with the bags. Let them discover how objects will fall out of the bags. Bring out other items that have holes in them, such as an old pair of socks or a box. Let the children discover the holes. Next, go on a walk to look for holes—a drain in a sink, a knothole in a fence, and so on. For a treat, give them each a small doughnut and have them look through the hole before eating it.

**3** Put blocks, items for a pretend picnic, books, or anything else that you want to emphasize into a pillowcase. Have your children try to guess what is in it. Show them the items and let them play with them. Use the pillowcase to introduce a new toy or to renew interest in a toy or a play center that has not been used for a while.

**4** Toddlers enjoy exploring light, darkness, and shadows. Bring a slide projector or an overhead projector into your room, and project a beam of light onto a plain white wall or a sheet of white paper taped to a wall. Let your children explore their shadows as they are projected onto the wall. Can they make their shadows dance? Jump? Hold hands with a friend?

**5** Make red and yellow ice cubes by adding food coloring to the water before freezing it. Put one ice cube of each color into a glass and let your children watch them melt and blend, making the color orange. Make ice cubes of various colors and let your children combine their own ice cubes to make different colors.

**6** Young children love going on "treasure hunts." One way to do this is to hide paper shapes all over the room or outdoors. Give each child a bag and let them put all the shapes they find in the bag. Toddlers also love to find plastic Easter eggs, colorful pompoms, and other small treasures. Be sure to have plenty so each child can find several.

**7** Set aside an area of the playground for a garden. Let your children dig in the dirt. Help them plant flowers and vegetables (radishes, carrots, and lettuce grow quickly). Provide watering pots so they can help water the seeds and plants. If you don't have space on the playground, let your children plant seeds in long window boxes placed on the ground.

**8** After a big snow, bring a dishpan of snow indoors. Let your children explore the cold, white stuff until it melts. You may want to have several dishpans of snow available, each one at a slightly different melting point.

**9** When you are ready for the mess, your toddlers will be ready to play in the mud. Fill several dishpans with dirt. Help your toddlers add some water, and then use their hands to mix it all up. Talk about the way the mud feels and what it does. When they are finished playing with the mud, have them make mud handprints on a white sheet of paper.

**10** Bring in a variety of cardboard tubes. Let your children experiment with them. Can they look through them? What will fit inside a tube? If you are lucky, you may be able to find a cardboard tube large enough for a child to fit through.

# Dramatic Play

# Creative Drama

**1** Toddlers love to move around and imitate familiar things in their lives. They like to pretend they are animals, babies, grownups, firefighters, and so on. Regularly encourage this natural skill and ability with individual children and with the whole group.

**2** Play a magic wand game. Have your children curl up into balls on the floor. Wave your "magic wand" (a cardboard tube, a ruler, a drinking straw, etc.) and say "Magic Wand, Magic Wand, turn these children into dogs." Have your children pretend to be dogs, crawling and barking as they move around. As soon as they hear you say "Magic Wand" again, have them curl up and listen for the next direction.

**3** Show your toddlers a rag doll. Encourage them to make their bodies limp like the doll's. How would they walk like a rag doll? Swim? Dance?

**4** Have your toddlers pretend to harvest fruits and vegetables. Can they stand up on their tiptoes to pick apples? Can they dig in the dirt to find potatoes?

**5** Ask your children to pretend to be birds, just learning how to fly. First, have them flap their wings slowly, then faster and faster. Soon they will be "flying" all over the room.

**6** Let your children pretend they are friendly monsters. Have them stomp around the room and growl "Hello" to everyone.

**7** Have your children walk on their knees as they pretend to be airplanes flying all around. Can they swoop around a corner? Can they zoom past you? When they are ready to land, have them slowly drop to the floor.

**8** Let your children pretend to take baths. Have them turn on the water, step into the bathtub, turn off the water, splash around, wash their bodies, step out of the tub, and dry themselves off.

**9** Designate an area in your room as the beehive. Have your children pretend to be bees, flying out to flowers, collecting the nectar, and flying home to the hive.

**10** Have your children pretend that their hands are sticky. Tell them that their hands stick to anything they touch. The only way they can get loose is if you pour pretend water over their hands.

# Movement Props

**4** A drum can encourage a variety of movements. Have your children move around the room as you beat a drum slowly. Gradually beat the drum faster and let your children try to keep up. Vary the drumbeats to encourage different kinds of movement.

**5** Tape crepe-paper strips to the sleeves of your toddlers' clothing to make wings. Take the children outside and let them float and fly all around.

**1** Bring in a bright light, such as a slide projector, shine it on a wall, and dim the lights. Let your children enjoy this light prop, dancing and moving in front of it to cast shadows on the wall.

**2** Boxes make wonderful props. They can become trains, special hideaways, and cars for dolls. Put out a box with a lid big enough for one child to hide inside. Have one of your children climb into the box and put the lid down. Tell the child to jump out of the box whenever he or she is ready to be a jack-in-the-box.

**3** Scarves are another useful movement prop. Have a box of scarves available. (You can purchase secondhand scarves at garage sales or thrift stores. You can also ask parents to donate ones they no longer wear.) All kinds of scarves work well. Encourage your children to use the scarves as they dance and move to music.

**9** Set an old mattress on the floor for your children to explore. It can become a boat in the middle of the ocean, a cloud floating by, a trampoline to jump on.

**10** Young children love plastic flower leis. They like to wear them, put them on dolls, and move them around as they dance to music.

**6** Another way to use crepe paper is to cut it into 2-foot strips. Staple six strips together at one end and cover the staples with masking tape. Make one of these for each child. Let your children make their streamers move up and down and all around as you play some music.

**7** Ankle bells are a great way to encourage movement. Purchase a set of ankle bells or make your own out of pipe cleaners and jingle bells. Children love to wear the bells on their ankles while they dance, walk, run, and move all around. Because this activity gets a little noisy, you may want to do it outdoors.

**8** Masking tape on the floor can be a wonderful movement prop. Stick the tape on the floor to make a design, such as a zigzag or a curvy line, a circle, a triangle, or a star. Let your children move along, over, and around the lines as they please.

# Music

**1** Enhance your children's dramatic play with music. Collect music in a variety of moods, rhythms, and beats. Have holiday music on hand, too. Play appropriate music as you do various movement and drama activities.

**2** Put on some music and invite your children to dance along with you. Encourage them to come up with a variety of ways to move to the music. This is a wonderful way for young children to express themselves. It is also a lot of fun and great for practicing large motor skills.

**3** Another way to include music in your children's dramatic play time is to introduce them to musical games. Traditional favorites such as Ring Around the Rosie and the Hokey-Pokey are still great ways to get children moving.

**4** Remember to let toddlers make their own music. Rhythm instruments such as drums, shakers, and bells work well with this age group. As always, be sure you have enough instruments so that each child can have his or her own.

**5** You can also make your own rhythm instruments. Empty coffee cans with the plastic lids on them make great drums. Rice or dried beans in plastic jars with the lids screwed on tight make great shakers. Sew jingle bells onto 3-inch circles cut out of heavy fabric to make shaking bells.

**6** Stay away from instruments that are put in the mouth to be played, such as toy horns, recorders, and kazoos, to avoid spreading germs.

**7** Tape various sounds of nature, such as the wind blowing, a dog barking, and frogs croaking. Let your children listen to the sounds and act out the motions.

**8** Securely fasten large jingle bells to your toddlers' shoes and let them make music as they dance around.

**9** Select action songs to sing with your children, such as "Skip to My Lou" or "Row, Row, Row Your Boat." Act out the motions together.

**10** Play this very simple version of Musical Chairs with your children. When the music starts, have them dance around. When the music stops, have them sit down on the floor.

# Home Life Center

**1** The home life center is especially important for toddlers because it offers opportunities for them to explore and experiment with a familiar part of their lives—living in a home and being a part of a family.

**2** Your children will want to pretend to prepare and eat food. Be sure to have a sturdy kitchen set, pretend food, and a child-size table with two to four chairs. You may also want to have a doll-size high chair.

**3** Select a good set of toy dishes for your children to use. Be sure the dishes are made out of a sturdy plastic and not out of glass or breakable plastic. Have enough so that each child playing in the center can have his or her own place setting of plate, cup, glass, and bowl.

**4** Omit the silverware for toddlers. Even plastic silverware can be dangerous. It is so easy for a child to fall with a spoon in his or her hand and get hurt. Also, toddlers want to put the silverware in their mouths, and it is just too difficult to keep the silverware sanitary.

**5** A play telephone is an important piece of equipment for your home life center. Have one that is sized right for a toddler. You may even want to have more than one phone so they can talk to each other or to you.

**8** Put a few baskets in your home life center. Baskets with handles are especially fun. Your children will enjoy putting things into the baskets and carrying them around.

**9** Collect empty food boxes (single-serving sizes work best). Stuff the boxes with crumpled newspaper and tape them shut. Your children will have fun playing with the boxes in the home life center.

**10** Try putting a small, easy-to-open suitcase in the home life center. Toddlers who have been on trips or have parents that travel will enjoy pretend play about packing, leaving, and coming home.

**6** Set out just a few items at a time in your home life center. If there are too many choices, you may find your toddlers dumping out a box of dishes or throwing plastic food instead of playing and interacting with them.

**7** Include a doll bed and doll blankets for your toddlers to play with and use to take care of doll babies in your home life center.

# Dress-Up Clothes

**1** Toddlers need dress-up clothes. By dressing up, they exercise imaginations and practice dressing themselves.

**2** Make sure that the dress-up clothes you choose for your toddlers go on and come off easily. They should be very simple, without many fancy zippers, buttons, or hooks.

**3** The tops, shirts, and jackets of preteen children are just the right size for toddlers' dress-up clothes. You can also make simple elastic-band skirts that are very simple for young children to put on and take off.

**4** Watch the length of dress-up clothing. Toddlers can trip easily on clothes that are too long. Simply cut off dresses and pants to make them just the right length.

**5** To add to your dress-up collection, ask parents if they have any old clothes or fabric they could donate, or check garage sales and thrift stores for inexpensive additions.

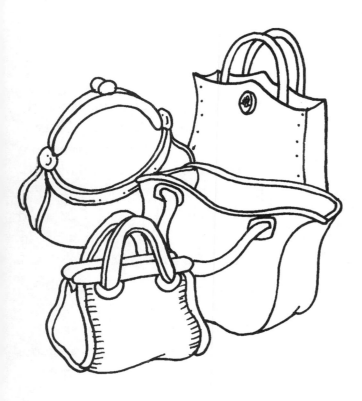

**9** Select low-heeled shoes for your dress-up collection. Look for shoes that are big enough to fit over a toddler's own shoes, but not so big that he or she trips while walking. A woman's size 6 works well for this age group.

**10** Hang a full-length mirror on the wall so your children can see themselves dressed up.

**6** When putting together your room's dress-up collection, be sure that you include a variety of clothes that would appeal to boys as well as girls. A pre-teen's old suit jacket and a clip tie are good.

**7** Be sure your dress-up collection also includes an assortment of purses. Select purses with handles that are small enough for your children to carry around. Also, check the latches to be sure that they won't pinch little fingers.

**8** One way to easily store and display dress-up clothes is to hang everything on hooks at your children's eye level. This makes the clothes easy for the children to see—there's no rummaging through a box—and it makes cleanup much easier for everyone.

# Playing With Dolls

**3** Doll clothing is optional. Toddlers will immediately undress the dolls. Then they will play with them, so clothes are not really necessary. If you do decide to have clothes, simple outfits with no small buttons or snaps are best, and be prepared to do most of the dressing, as toddlers usually do not have the skill to dress their dolls yet.

**4** Children enjoy having blankets for their dolls. They wrap up their dolls and carry them around. They spread their blankets on the floor and put their dolls on them. A baby's receiving blanket cut into fourths is just the right size. You can also use an old clean kitchen dishcloth.

**5** Your toddlers will want to put their dolls to bed. Small cardboard boxes make perfect cradles, as do large plastic containers.

**1** The dolls in the toddler room should be soft baby-doll types that are not too big and not too small. They should be just right for toddlers to carry around and take care of. Be sure you have boy dolls and girl dolls.

**2** Select dolls with the thought of washing them on a daily basis. Dolls get so much use that this is a necessity, especially with toddlers. Dolls with molded hair hold up better than those with rooted hair.

**9** Sturdy paper towels and strips of masking tape make great diapers for dolls.

**10** Doll high chairs are a real favorite with this age group. You may want to have more than one.

**6** To make a wagon for a doll, attach a short length of string to the front of a cardboard box. Show your children how to pull the box along the floor to take a doll for a ride.

**7** Reserve a special time on the indoor climber and slide for your children to take their dolls "to the park." Let the children take turns pushing their dolls down the slide. You could also make a swing out of a bucket with a handle.

**8** Toddlers love to push their babies around in strollers. Try to have at least two or three doll strollers for your children to use.

# Impromptu Centers

**1** Impromptu centers are play centers that are quickly created by the teacher and enjoyed as long as the toddlers are interested. The possibilities are endless, but here are a few suggestions.

**2** Put a large blanket or a sheet over a table to create a house or a tent. Crawl into the house with your children. Let them bring in whatever toys they want. It is fun to just sit inside of it and talk, too.

**3** Fold a large blanket in half and arrange it on the floor. Pretend that the blanket is a boat. Let your children sit on the boat and pretend to go fishing or have them rock back and forth as they pretend the boat is going really fast.

**4** Spread out a blanket on the floor to create a picnic area. Bring some dishes and some imaginary food, too.

**5** Set up chairs in a long line to make a train or a bus. Have the driver sit in the first chair. Invite your toddlers to join you on this ride. Encourage them to bring their dolls along, if they like.

**6** Set out grocery bags, play food, and some paper money for a quick shopping trip with your children.

**7** Collect some old newspapers. Let your children pretend to deliver them to all the houses in the neighborhood. Then have them sit down and pretend to read the news.

**9** Set up a large appliance box in the center of the room. It can become a tunnel, a cave, or a house.

**10** Set up an inflatable boat for your children to "sail" in. They will want to fill the boat with all their treasures.

**8** Set out a bin of paper of various kinds. Let your toddlers "write" letters, put them in envelopes, and pretend to mail them. They can make grocery lists. They can make tickets for the circus. They will amaze you with their creativity.

# Movement Games

**1** Play Follow the Leader with your children. Turn on some music and lead them around the room as you walk, jump, dance, crawl, and twirl around.

**2** Draw a clown face with a wide-open mouth on a large cardboard box. Cut out the clown's mouth. Give your children beanbags. Let them "feed the clown" by tossing the beanbags into the clown's mouth.

**3** Pretend to be an animal trainer. Have your children pretend to be dogs or any other animal you agree on. Instruct your "animals" to follow your directions, such as "Roll over. Run around the room. Sit up. Jump up and down."

**4** Play this copycat game with your children. Position your body in a certain way and ask the children to copy you. Start with simple positions, such as one arm in the air, and move on to more complex ones, such as kneeling on the floor with one hand on your hip and one hand on your shoulder. Repeat as long as interest lasts.

**5** Choose one child to play this game with you. Give the child a cardboard tube to hold like a baseball bat. Crumple up a sheet of newspaper and toss it at the tube. Encourage the child to swing at the ball.

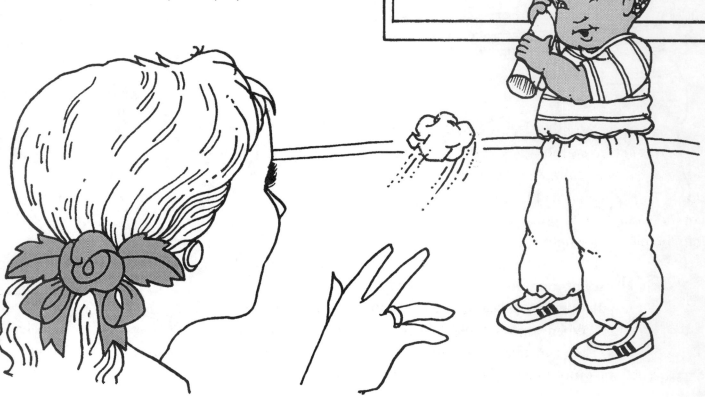

**6** Let your children act out the nursery rhyme of Jack and Jill. Recite the rhyme while they pretend to climb a hill carrying a bucket. Have them fall down like Jack, then roll across the floor like Jill rolled down the hill. If you have a hill, it is even more fun to let your children roll down that.

**7** Set out sheets of newspaper and a large pillowcase. Show your children how to crumple up the newspaper and stuff it into the pillowcase. Encourage them to crumple the newspaper quickly, slowly, noisily, quietly, with their feet, and so on. Let them continue to put crumpled newspaper into the pillowcase until it is full.

**8** Have your children pretend to be wiggle worms and wiggle around the room. When you say "Stop," have them stop wiggling. When you say "Go," have them start again.

**9** Let your children pretend to travel in various kinds of vehicles. Sing the following song, substituting the name and action of another vehicle for *Drive, drive, drive my car.*

*Sung to: "Row, Row, Row Your Boat"*

Drive, drive, drive my car,
I drive it here and there.
I love to drive my special car,
I drive it everywhere.

*Gayle Bittinger*

**10** Play this cookie cutter game with your children. Have them pretend to be cookie dough and lie on the floor. Use a round bolster pillow or a large cardboard tube and "roll" them out flat. Shake pretend sugar sprinkles all over them and "bake" them in the oven. When the cookies are done, pretend to eat them all up!

# Encouraging Dramatic Play

**1** Be sure not to inadvertently limit your children's choices. There are no "little girl" or "little boy" toys. There are only toys for everyone. Encourage boys to play in the home life center and girls to play with blocks. One way to do this is to keep your areas as interesting as possible for both. If you put firefighter hats in the home life center, chances are that both boys and girls will wear them. Add toy people or animals to the block area, and boys and girls will expand their block play.

**2** When you play with your toddlers, you model dramatic-play behaviors—wrapping up a doll, talking on the telephone, pushing a truck, setting up some animals. This is a valuable learning opportunity for toddlers.

**3** Modeling appropriate dramatic-play behaviors also gives your children the opportunity to observe and experience cooperative play. The more opportunities they have to do this, the more likely they will play in this way when they are developmentally ready.

**4** Sitting down and playing with your children has the additional benefit of extending the children's play time and helping their attention spans grow a little.

**5** When you are playing with your children in active dramatic play, let them take the lead. You may suggest, "Let's put the babies to bed." You may have planned on putting them in the baby cradle, but if they want to put the babies to bed in the refrigerator because it looks like a bunk bed, let them do that. Modeling appropriate behaviors and giving them the freedom to explore and play requires a careful balancing.

**6** When maintenance workers come to your place, point them out to your children. Encourage the children to pretend to mow the grass or wash the windows as they saw the workers do.

**7** Take your children places where they can watch people in action. A trip to the fire station can encourage lots of firefighter play. A visit to the grocery store may inspire cooking and shopping play. Give your children experiences that they can remember and build on in their play.

**8** Make your dramatic-play materials easily accessible. If they are easy to find and easy to get out, your children will be more likely to use them. Arrange items on a shelf rather than in a box. Or, keep the items in see-through boxes so your children can easily identify the contents.

**9** Change things around regularly to spark your children's interest in dramatic play. Rearrange the home life center. Put your dress-up clothes out on the table one morning. Put new play food on the stove. Set out a bucket and a soft, dry sponge. Think of other ways to incorporate your children's experiences into their dramatic play.

**10** Encourage parents to come in to your classroom and share real-life tools of their trades. If possible, let them demonstrate some of the things they do on their jobs. For example, a parent who works in retail could bring in a cash register till, a bookkeeper could show the children an adding machine, a nurse could bring in a real stethoscope, and so on.

# Small Motor Play

# Selecting and Using Manipulatives

**1** Invest in good quality materials. It may seem like a lot of money to spend right up front, but the investment will more than pay for itself as your manipulatives withstand use by young children day after day after day.

**2** Choose well-constructed materials, ones with pieces that fit together well and are easy to manipulate.

**3** Make a commitment to eventually buy enough equipment for each child to have his or her own set. Being patient and waiting for a turn are difficult for toddlers. Provide enough blocks, beads, etc., for each child to work successfully.

**4** Before you buy materials, check for overall safety. Are there any sharp edges? Are the pieces too big for a toddler to swallow or choke on? Also, be sure to check the materials in your room periodically to make sure they remain safe.

**5** Select equipment that can withstand a lot of washing. Paperboard products are difficult to clean. Wood and plastic equipment is better suited for this age group.

**8** One way to encourage the use of a variety of table toys is to set out just one toy at a table. Sit with your children as they experiment and figure out what to do. As their interest wanes and they go on to other things, put that table toy away and get out another one.

**9** You may find that at the end of a play time, several different sets of manipulatives have gotten mixed up. Make the cleanup of the toys a game, and have your children help you sort them.

**10** Involve your children in the care of the manipulatives. When it is time to wash them, let the children help. Fill a bucket with warm, soapy water and let the children scrub and clean the toys.

**6** Limit the number of manipulative toys that are available at any one time. Too many choices are confusing for young children and can make it more difficult for them to choose an activity.

**7** Just sitting on the floor next to toddlers as they work with manipulatives can encourage them. Refrain from directing their play or asking too many questions. Let them explore the manipulatives on their own. As you watch them work, however, be ready to step in and offer a little assistance if their frustration level gets too high.

# Table Blocks

**1** Small building blocks are as valuable today as they have always been for young children's play. Select square wooden blocks that are all the same size or have a set of blocks that includes squares, rectangles, columns, and arches. The blocks should be too large for a toddler to swallow or choke on.

**2** Table blocks of various colors can be stacked up, lined up, or arranged by color. Other blocks toddlers enjoy are bristle blocks, large interlocking blocks, and magnetic blocks.

**3** When introducing your children to blocks, take the time to sit and play with them. Telling them to "go play with the blocks" is not enough. They need some guidance and a little hands-on experience with you.

**4** Children usually do not build with blocks immediately. In the beginning, your toddlers may just want to carry the blocks around or put them in trucks to haul them from one place to another. Then they may decide to create a road with the blocks by placing them on the table in a long line.

**5** When your children are ready to build with the blocks, you may notice that their creations tend to follow this progression: first they will build small towers, then larger towers, then one-block-high walls, then higher walls.

**9** Homemade blocks are also fun for toddlers. Tape the ends of small, square cardboard boxes securely closed and glue colorful pictures to the sides. Cover the boxes with clear self-stick paper for durability. Let your children play with these blocks, stacking and arranging them. Encourage them to incorporate the pictures on the blocks into their play.

**10** Empty facial tissue boxes make great blocks. Your toddlers will love putting small toys through the hole in each box as much as they will like stacking the boxes.

**6** Small blocks can be used on the floor or on a table. The most important consideration is that each child has his or her own blocks and enough space to build in. You may want to establish a few ground rules for block play, such as never take another child's blocks and only the builder can knock down his or her creation.

**7** Keep blocks available to your toddlers by storing them in containers that are easy for a child to reach. Put enough blocks in each container so that a child has enough to build with, but not so many that cleanup is too difficult.

**8** When purchasing interlocking plastic blocks, do not mix brands. They are not easily interchangeable, and toddlers get frustrated when a tower tips over because one of the blocks just does not fit right. Many block manufacturers offer a variety of accessories to use with their blocks. Most toddlers do not have the skill to use them appropriately. These accessories are better suited for older children.

# Puzzles

**1** Puzzles are wonderful manipulatives. The best ones are those made out of wood or plastic. Cardboard puzzles are not sturdy enough or washable enough to withstand regular toddler use.

**2** Toddlers enjoy puzzles with familiar pictures on them. Look for puzzles of animals, toys, clothes, people, or vehicles. Scenic puzzles are better for older children.

**3** Make sure each puzzle is simple, with no more than eight pieces, and that the pieces are large enough for a toddler to handle. Puzzles that have frames are better than those that do not. The simplest puzzles have single pieces that fit into their own shapes. It is best to start with these and move on to puzzles with pieces that interlock.

**4** As your children sit down to work on puzzles, be sure each child has his or her own puzzle. Let your children explore, but be ready to offer help if they are struggling and about to get too frustrated. Puzzles challenge young children mentally and physically and stretch new skills to the limit.

**5** No matter what precautions you take, some puzzles will get dumped out on the floor. To make it easier to clean up, make sure each puzzle is marked as follows. Each time you add a puzzle to your collection, select a letter or number for that puzzle and write it on the back of each piece with a permanent marker. This way, when several puzzles are dumped out, you will know which pieces go to which puzzle.

**6** If you find your puzzles being dumped on the floor too often, consider storing them on a high shelf. Do remember to take one or two down frequently for your children to work on.

**7** Toddlers love handmade puzzles to take home. And while these puzzles won't withstand the daily use they might receive from a group of children, they last for quite a while at home.

**8** Have your children color on sheets of construction paper. Cover each child's paper with clear self-stick paper, and then cut it into three or four simple puzzle pieces. Put each child's pieces into a resealable plastic bag to take home.

**9** Take a photo of each of your children, glue it to a piece of posterboard, and cover it with clear self-stick paper. Cut each photo into two or three simple puzzle pieces and put the pieces into a resealable plastic bag for the child to take home.

**10** Play this puzzle game with your children. Buy a set of cardboard holiday decorations. Cut each picture into two pieces, creating a mini-puzzle. Give each child one of the puzzle pieces. Have the children look at each other's puzzle pieces to try to find the one that fits into theirs.

# Sorting Toys

**1** Sorting toys are very easy to make. You can use an assortment of almost any small item and a container such as a basket, a plastic jar, or a box. For safety, check that any items you use are too big for a toddler to swallow or choke on.

**2** Give each toddler his or her own container and several items for sorting. Sit at the table with your children, with your own container. Play alongside the children, putting one item at a time into your container, and talking about what you and they are doing. This activity, putting in items one at a time, is the very first toddler sorting activity.

**3** Toddlers love dropping clothespins into a plastic container or moving pompoms from one container to another with kitchen tongs.

**4** A basket is great fun for sorting. Your children will enjoy putting objects into the basket and taking them out again.

**5** Cut a square hole in the plastic lid of a large empty container. Show your toddlers how to push small blocks through the hole.

**9** Collect three toy cars and three stuffed toy animals. Mix up the cars and animals, and then have your children sort them into two separate piles. This works with any two kinds of toys or materials you have. As your children become more skilled at this, you can increase the difficulty by having them sort two similar items such as toy cars and toy trucks.

**10** Toddlers love this color sorting activity. Set out two sheets of construction paper: one red and one blue. Find three red toys and three blue toys. Let your children place the red toys on the red construction paper and the blue toys on the blue paper. Help the children say the color of each toy as they put it on the paper. Repeat with any other colors you wish to introduce to your children.

**6** For older toddlers, you can make a sorting box by cutting a square hole and a round hole in the lid of a shoebox. Put the lid on the box and let your children put empty thread spools through the round hole in the lid and square blocks through the square hole.

**7** Have each child take off one shoe and put it in the middle of the room. When all the shoes are piled up, let your children sort through them to find their own shoes.

**8** Put out a variety of items in big and little sizes: socks, plates, and books. Let your children put the big items in a big basket and the little items in a little basket.

# Nesting and Stacking Toys

**1** When choosing nesting and stacking toys for your toddlers, look for those that have only a few pieces. Toys with too many pieces to figure out can frustrate toddlers.

**2** Make a nesting game for your children by collecting paper cups in three or four different sizes. Place the cups, right side up, on a table. Show the children how to place the cups inside one another, starting with the largest cup. A set of measuring cups also works well.

**3** Boxes make a nice nesting game. Set out three or four boxes in different sizes for your children to nest together.

**4** Purchase plastic eggs in small, medium, and large sizes. Put one of each size together to make a fun nesting toy for spring.

**5** A nesting set of pots makes a great toy. Your toddlers will love experimenting with them to find out just how they can nest together.

**6** Toddlers especially enjoy stacking rings. You can purchase commercially made stacking rings or you can make your own. A small bathroom plunger and some shower curtain rings or large metal canning jar rings make a fun game.

**7** You can also make a stacking rings game out of a wooden bottle-drying rack and some old napkin rings. Have your children put the rings on the dowels of the bottle-drying rack.

**9** Collect several small plastic containers that are all the same size. Let your children stack and unstack them.

**10** For an unusual stacking game, collect plastic cups and saucers. Show your children how to stack them by alternating saucers and cups, then let them try to make a two- or three-cup tower.

**8** Make a different kind of stacking toy by cutting the tops and bottoms off plastic 1- or 2-liter bottles to make cylinders. Cover the cylinders with self-stick paper, if you wish. Show your children how to stack the cylinders on top of each other.

# Stringing Activities

**3** Make sure each child has a string with a "stopper" of some sort at one end and a "needle" at the other. It also helps if you select yarn or string that is not too slippery, so that the beads do not easily slide off.

**4** To make a "needle" at one end of the string, wrap it with a small piece of masking tape.

**5** Instead of using string, you can use colorful pipe cleaners. Because pipe cleaners are stiffer, they are sometimes easier for beginning "stringers" to use. The ends of pipe cleaners can be sharp, so be sure to supervise.

**1** Large beads, such as those used for macrame and found at craft stores, work well for stringing activities. Be sure the beads are too large for toddlers to swallow or choke on. Also keep the length of all lacing strings to 12 inches or less. Supervise stringing activities at all times.

**2** Toddlers really enjoy threading beads onto yarn. They may want to put only a few beads on each piece of yarn or they may want to fill up the entire length. Toddlers are not interested in creating patterns with different colors or shapes of beads. For them, the joy is in the process of stringing.

**9** Cut out the egg cups in an egg carton and punch a hole in the bottom of each one. These egg cups make great beginning beads, perfect for stringing on yarn.

**10** Cut interesting shapes out of plastic milk containers and plastic lids. Punch a small hole in the middle of each shape and let your children use them for stringing.

**6** Spools and large shoelaces are great beginning stringing materials. If you are using wooden spools, you can even have your toddlers paint them a day or two before they are used for stringing.

**7** Toddlers enjoy making necklaces by stringing onto yarn 1-inch pieces of plastic drinking straws and paper shapes with holes poked in the middle.

**8** Toddlers like to string O-shaped cereal onto strings to make necklaces they can eat.

# Sewing and Weaving

**1** Once your toddlers have had experience with stringing, they are ready to try some simple sewing cards. At this point, don't worry about using any particular kind of stitch. The in-and-out movement of the yarn and "needle" through the holes in the sewing cards is the important thing.

**2** A shoelace with plastic-coated ends makes the best string for any sewing card. You can tie one end to one of the holes on the sewing card and your children can use the other end as a needle.

**3** If you don't have shoelaces, make a "needle" on short lengths of string or yarn by dipping the ends in glue and letting them dry overnight before using them.

**4** You can make a sewing card from an old vinyl placemat. Cut a large shape, such as an animal, a fish, or a piece of fruit, from the placemat. Use a hole punch to punch holes at regular intervals around the edge of the shape. Tie a shoelace to one of the holes and the sewing card is ready.

**5** The fronts of sturdy greeting cards also make interesting sewing cards. Leave the card as is or cut around an interesting shape and make the sewing card out of that. Punch holes around the edges and tie on a string or a shoelace for sewing.

**9** Hang a net, such as a badminton or a volleyball net, on a wall. Make sure the top of the net is securely attached. Set out a basket of long fabric scraps, strips of paper, lengths of ribbon, and so on. Let your children weave the materials in and out of the net.

**10** Yarn wraps on simple cardboard shapes are a very simple sewing activity. To do this, cut shapes out of cardboard and cut several slits around the edge of each one. Show your toddlers how to wrap yarn around the shapes by sliding it between the slits.

**6** Cut a large shape out of a clean plastic-foam tray. Punch holes around the edge of the shape and attach a shoelace or string to make another kind of sewing card.

**7** Punch holes around the edge of a colorful paper plate to make a round sewing card. You can use holiday plates to make holiday sewing cards.

**8** For a simple weaving experience, tie a length of ribbon to a laundry basket that has vertical slits in it. Show your children how to weave the ribbon in and out of the slits.

# Pegboards and Pounding Boards

**1** Toddlers like pegs and pegboards. Select pegboards with pegs that fit into them easily but also securely. Be sure the pegs are large enough to prevent them from being swallowed or choked on.

**2** Toddlers are not interested in using pegs to make patterns. They just like to fill up the pegboard with pegs.

**3** You can also set out lumps of modeling dough and pegs. Your children will enjoy pushing the pegs into the dough.

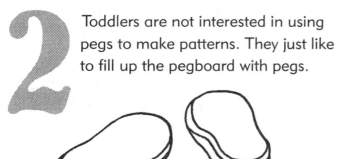

**4** You can make this simple, beginning pegboard out of a shoebox and empty toilet tissue tubes. Cut two 2-inch circles out of the lid of the shoebox to make the "pegboard." Let one of your children put the cardboard tube "pegs" in the holes. You can make a set of these for each child.

**5** Toddlers love playing with this toy, another simple, beginning pegboard. Cut four slits in the top of a shoebox lid. Set out the box and four craft sticks. Let your children put the craft sticks in and out of the slits.

**6** Small pounding benches are a good small motor toy. Have several so that more than one child at a time can pound. Remind the children that only the pegs are to be pounded, not people or other toys.

**7** Let your children use child-size hammers to pound golf tees into blocks of plastic-foam packing material.

**8** Your children will enjoy using a lightweight wooden hammer to pound drinking straw sections into modeling dough.

**9** Turn an egg carton upside down and poke a hole in each egg cup. Place the egg carton on the table upside down and set out 12 crayons. Let your children place one crayon in each egg-cup hole.

**10** Fill a fairly deep pan with dirt or modeling dough. Let your children pound craft sticks into the dirt or dough.

# Transportation Toys

**3** Select simple toys without a lot of movable parts. Be sure that the wheels or other parts cannot come off easily and present a choking hazard. Battery-operated toys or fragile model vehicles are not appropriate for toddlers.

**4** Toddlers love to be able to carry their toys around. Be sure to have some transportation toys that are small enough for this activity.

**1** Transportation toys include trucks, cars, planes, and trains. When buying these toys, it helps to buy them in identical pairs. This makes it a little easier for toddlers who want the same toy but don't usually want to share.

**2** Choose transportation toys made out of wood or plastic. Many metal toys have sharp points that can hurt young children.

**5** Transportation toys require a lot of floor space. It is best if you can have an area that is set aside solely for this kind of play to avoid children being run into and toys crashing into other things.

**8** Make tunnels for your children to drive their vehicles through. A large opening cut in opposite sides of an upside-down box makes a great tunnel. So does a 12-inch length of a wide cardboard tube.

**9** Toddlers are fascinated by trains. Add one or two to your transportation area. Small trains that are held together by magnets or ones that hook together are favorites. You can have a simple round track available, but young children usually prefer pushing the trains around on the floor.

**6** You can make "roads" for your children to drive their vehicles on by sticking masking tape on the floor in a line. Show them how to push their cars along the "road."

**10** Don't forget to take transportation toys out to the dirt or to a sandbox for a completely different experience.

**7** Setting out plastic toy people and animals in the transportation area can add a whole new element to your children's play.

# Large Motor Play

# Walking and Running

**1** Walking and running are very important to toddlers. They have just learned to walk and they want to practice this new skill. Wise teachers build upon this need and channel it into safe and appropriate activities. Your children will appreciate as much freedom to explore this new skill as you can give them.

**2** It is tempting to carry a toddler when you are headed to a particular destination, especially if you are in a hurry. Try to resist the temptation as much as you possibly can. Any opportunity for a toddler to walk instead of being carried provides good practice and is a good habit to get into.

**3** Because toddlers want to run around outside, be sure they have a safe surface, like grass or sand, to run on. This is important because toddlers are not steady on their feet just yet.

**4** Applauding your children on their ability to pick themselves up again after a stumble, even if they are initially upset, helps to focus attention away from the fall itself. Complimenting toddlers when they pick themselves up changes falling from a bad experience to a better one, and will make future falls less frightening.

**5** Toddlers love to chase adults. Be sure to provide enough space and opportunity for this activity. If you are playing a chasing game inside, arrange the furniture so you have an open space.

**6** To encourage your children to test out their running legs, suggest various destinations for them to run to. For example, you could say, "Let me see you run to the slide," or "Can you run to the big tree?"

**7** Pull toys and push toys can really encourage your children's running and walking. Toddlers love to push a toy grocery cart or a toy lawn mower in front of them or pull a toy dog with a wagging tail behind them. Push toys can also steady the walk of toddlers and give them more control. Commercially bought push toys are a favorite, but children will also push chairs, boxes, and milk crates across the linoleum or outside.

**8** Crepe-paper streamers, cut into 2-foot lengths, are a perfect tool for encouraging walking and running. Toddlers can hold the streamers while they walk and let them drag on the floor, or they can run and make the streamers "fly."

**9** If you are walking somewhere with a group of toddlers, get a length of sturdy rope and tie knots in it, each knot about 2 feet apart. Hold up the rope and have each child hang on to a different knot. Ask them to continue holding on to their knot as you walk to your destination, together and in a fairly straight line.

**10** Children love to walk or march in a parade. Have them parade around your room as you play marching music. Or, sing the following song as they walk to the next activity.

*Sung to: "Frère Jacques"*

We are marching,
We are marching—
Here and there, everywhere.
We are marching quickly.
We are marching slowly.
March, march, march.
March, march, march.

*Gayle Bittinger*

# Crawling and Climbing

**1** Toddlers climb onto adult-size chairs and couches, in and out of cribs or beds, over safety nets, and wherever else they can. Encourage the development of this skill by providing many climbing opportunities throughout the day. Let them climb into your lap, instead of being lifted into it, to hear a story. Take a little extra time to let them climb up stairs. When your toddlers practice climbing, they are really practicing coordination and balance and strengthening their muscles, too.

**2** By the time they are toddlers, crawling is getting to be second nature to most of your children. Add a little twist by varying the materials they crawl on. Let them crawl on a tile floor, a carpeted floor, a mat or a pillow, or the grass outside.

**3** Help your toddlers play Follow the Leader as they crawl in circles or around the room. Set up a table to crawl under and a ramp to crawl over.

**4** Ask your toddlers to pretend to be a favorite animal while they crawl. Can they crawl and bark like a dog? What does a cat look like as it crawls around and meows?

**5** Have several different toy vehicles for your children to push as they crawl on the floor. Cars, buses, trucks, and airplanes are lots of fun.

**6** Place a ladder flat on the ground and let your toddlers practice stepping or climbing over the ladder rungs. Stand close by to help as needed.

**7** Wait until a child is ready to climb before encouraging him or her to explore a slide or a climber. When children are confident and eager to climb, then they usually have the physical skill to do it. Also, be ready to "rescue" beginning climbers—children who have learned to climb *up* but not down. Most children learn how to climb up before they learn how to climb down.

**8** A climber for toddlers should have wide steps that are close together with a rail to hang on to. The climber itself should not be more than 4 feet tall. If the climber is outside, it should have a cushion of sand or pea gravel under it to protect any child who might slip and fall.

**9** Children playing on a climber need close supervision. Standing close by also means you can lend a hand or steady a step to increase a child's confidence in his or her abilities and help the child be successful.

**10** Climbing stairs is an important part of your toddlers' development. If possible, provide your children with a sturdy, three-step toddler climber for practice indoors. As you watch your children practice on the stairs, you will notice these stages. Climbing up the stairs, they first crawl up the steps, then walk up them, one at a time. Going down the stairs is a little trickier for them. The first stage is crawling or sliding down the stairs backwards on their tummies. Next, they sit on the steps and scoot down one at a time. Finally, they start walking down the stairs, one stair at a time.

# Balancing

**1** Tiptoeing is an important balancing skill. Have your toddlers practice by having a tiptoe dance, tiptoeing while singing a song ("Tiptoe to My Lou"), or walking tiptoe to the snack table or other favorite destination.

**2** Another fun way to practice balance is to let your children "dress up" and walk in grown-up shoes. If the shoes have heels, limit the height to 1 or 2 inches.

**3** Toddlers enjoy walking and trying to balance on foam mats or pillows. Purchase simple foam mats, or stack pillows up and have your children balance as they shift their weight from one side to the other.

**4** Balancing on a ball is a fun activity for toddlers. Let your toddlers take turns lying across a large playground ball. Pull them toward you and then push them away. As they get used to this activity, they will be able to do it themselves by rolling forward and catching themselves with their hands, then pushing backward and catching themselves with their feet.

**5** Try the Stork Stand with your toddlers. Have each child find a chair or a table to hold on to with both hands. Ask them to each hold up one leg, just like a stork does. Next, have them hold on with only one hand and hold up their leg. Finally, encourage them to try balancing on one leg without holding on to anything.

**6** Let your toddlers do the "tape walk." Place a line of masking tape on the floor and let your children walk along the tape. After they have perfected that, place a rope on the floor and let them try walking on it.

**7** After your children are comfortable walking the tape, try a walking board. Find a 4-foot board that is 3 to 4 inches wide and ½ inch thick, and lay it on the floor. Let your children take turns walking along this board.

**8** Hold a child's hand as he or she walks along the walking board or a balance beam that is on the floor. This helps them practice and get the feel of balancing on the board or the beam. Let your children take turns walking sideways across the board. Can they walk to one end and turn around?

**9** As you watch your toddlers balance on the walking board, you will notice that they first begin with one foot on the board and one foot on the floor. This is normal. It takes a while to learn to walk on the board with both feet, and many toddlers are not able to do it just yet.

**10** Walking on a ramp or a hill helps young children practice their balance as they move uphill and downhill. Find a short hill or a small ramp for your children to practice on. You may need to initially hold your children's hands as they move up and down the ramp or hill.

# Jumping

**1** Jumping is a favorite toddler activity, and it lets them use up lots of energy. One way you can encourage jumping is to place several Hula Hoops on the floor. Have your toddlers practice jumping into and out of the hoops.

**2** Look around your room to find other safe items for your children to practice jumping over. A block placed on the floor is fun to jump over. So is a jump rope stretched out in a long line.

**3** Let your children play "Jack Be Nimble." Set an unlit votive candle on the floor. Select a child to jump over the candle. Substitute his or her name for *Jack* in the following rhyme.

Jack be nimble,
Jack be quick.
Jack jump over the candlestick.

*Traditional*

**4** Jumping up is a different skill from jumping over or across. Let your toddlers practice this kind of jumping with the following activity. Tie one end of a string to a foam ball. Tie the other end to a hook on the ceiling so that the ball hangs a few inches above your children's reach. Let your children jump up to try to touch the ball.

**5** Find several carpet squares. (Check with a local carpet store for free or inexpensive ones.) Arrange the carpet squares in a path around your room, making certain that the squares will not slip when your children jump on them. Show the toddlers how to jump from one square to the next to follow the path. If you like, have the path lead to the door before going outside or to some other destination.

**9** Have your children crouch down low. Tell them that when they feel your touch, they can jump up and try to touch the sky. If you wish, show the children a jack-in-the-box toy and have them pretend to be "Jack" as they jump up.

**10** Set a mattress on the floor and have your children jump up and down on it as if it were a trampoline. Depending on the size of the mattress, make sure that only two or three children jump at a time.

**6** Self-stick dots can also be used to create a path on the floor. Have your children follow the path by jumping from one dot to the next. Can they jump *over* any of the dots?

**7** Have your children pretend to be frogs or kangaroos as they hop all over the room or a playground.

**8** Set a sturdy, one-step step stool in the middle of your room. Arrange a pile of pillows on one side of the step stool. Have your children take turns climbing onto the step stool and jumping off it into the pile of pillows.

# Blocks and Balls

**1** Large block play helps your children develop their large muscles and coordination. The earliest stage of block play is to simply carry a block around. After a while, children begin to stack the blocks vertically or lay them on the floor in a line. As children get older and more skilled, the structures that they can build with blocks become increasingly complex.

**2** You may find that your toddlers are not quite sure what to do with blocks. Modeling block play for them, building a tower, or placing the blocks in a line on the floor is very important. A fun way to start is to let a child watch you lay blocks end to end on the floor to make a circle large enough for you to sit in. You might say, "This is my house. Would you like me to make a house for you?" Arrange more blocks in another circle, encouraging the child to help as he or she can.

**3** Large, lightweight building blocks are perfect for toddlers. Stuff empty diaper boxes or cereal boxes with crumpled newspaper and cover them with self-stick paper to make inexpensive blocks. Children love stacking these blocks and then knocking them over.

**4** Because knocking down a block structure is, for many toddlers, more fun than building it, having this simple rule is helpful: Only the child who built the structure may knock it down.

**5** Make your own lightweight blocks out of milk cartons. Collect an even number of clean milk cartons with the tops cut off. Stuff half of the cartons with crumpled newspaper. Slide an empty carton over each stuffed carton to make a block. These blocks are great for stacking and knocking down.

**6** Toddlers also need large, soft balls to play with, such as rubber balls, foam rubber balls, and balls of wadded paper. Hard balls, like basketballs and soccer balls, are best for older children because they can hurt toddlers. Be sure to have enough balls so that each child can have one.

**9** Let your toddlers practice throwing balls into a large cardboard box, a laundry basket, or another container.

**10** A great way to encourage ball play is to invite high school soccer and basketball players to do a demonstration for your group. For weeks after this show, your toddlers will try to copy the "big kids," kicking and bouncing their own rubber balls.

**7** A great activity for beginning ball play is to have a child throw his or her ball, run after it, and then pick it up and throw it again. A young child will play this game over and over.

**8** Encourage older toddlers to try to throw the ball to each other and catch it. To master this skill, have them first sit on the floor and roll the ball back and forth to each other. This helps them practice their aim, their catching skills, and the concept of taking turns.

# Beanbags

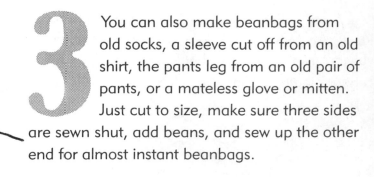

**3** You can also make beanbags from old socks, a sleeve cut off from an old shirt, the pants leg from an old pair of pants, or a mateless glove or mitten. Just cut to size, make sure three sides are sewn shut, add beans, and sew up the other end for almost instant beanbags.

**4** For variety, stuff your homemade beanbags with different textures, such as dried beans, macaroni, cotton balls, or salt. Help your children notice any differences in the way the various beanbags act when thrown or when dropped to the ground.

**5** Young children can be hard on beanbags. Check your beanbags daily for tears or rips. Repair or replace them as needed.

**1** For toddlers, beanbags can be less threatening and easier to catch than a ball. To practice tossing and catching a beanbag, have a child sit across from you. Gently toss a beanbag to him or her. Have the child toss the beanbag back to you.

**2** To make beanbags, select fabric in a variety of colors, patterns, and textures. Cut out two squares and sew them together on three sides. Fill the beanbags with large dried beans and stitch them securely closed.

**8** Take several beanbags to a small toddler slide. Invite one of your children to join you. Have the child roll or slide the beanbags down the slide while you catch them. Trade places with the child and have him or her try to catch the beanbags while you roll them down the slide.

**9** For balancing practice, place a beanbag on each child's head. Have your children carefully walk around the room while balancing the beanbags.

**10** For more balancing practice, ask your children to stand up. Place a small beanbag on one shoe of each child. Have the children try to walk around the room, keeping the beanbags on their shoes.

**6** For throwing practice, set out a laundry basket and some beanbags. To start, have your children stand beside the basket and just drop the beanbags into it. As their skills develop, have the children step back from the basket and throw the beanbags into it. Designating a target also helps set limits for indoor throwing, so beanbags are not being thrown at other children or things.

**7** Take the beanbags outside and let your children try to throw them up and over various things, such as a climber, a tree branch, or a swing.

# Blankets

**1** Use blankets to encourage your toddlers' large motor play. Collect several different sizes and kinds for them to play and experiment with. For example, you could have on hand a small, lightweight baby blanket; a large, heavy quilt; a crocheted throw; and a cozy cotton or nylon blanket.

**2** Arrange several blankets on the floor to make a "trail." Have your toddlers crawl along the trail. The trail could lead them under a table, around a chair, and through a box tunnel.

**3** Spread a blanket on the floor. Have several of your children sit on the floor around the edges of the blanket and put their legs underneath it. Have the children raise their legs off the ground to lift the blanket. How high can they raise the blanket?

**4** Arrange several small baby blankets on the floor. Place a stuffed animal on each blanket. Let your children use the blankets to pull the stuffed animals around the room.

**5** Older toddlers will enjoy using small blankets to "scoot" across a tile floor. Have each child sit on the edge of a blanket. Show the children how to use their feet to scoot themselves forward or backward.

**6** You can play this fun toss-and-catch game with one of your toddlers. Spread a small blanket on the floor and place a teddy bear in the middle of it. Show the child how to hold on to two of the blanket corners while you hold on to the other two. Together, lift the blanket off the floor, gently toss the bear into the air, and catch it in the blanket.

**7** Cover a table with a large quilt or a blanket to make a tent or a tunnel. Encourage your children to crawl in and out of the tent. If you like, have them pretend to be bears and growl as they crawl into their "bear cave."

**8** Find a blanket with a large checkered pattern or an old quilt made from squares. Spread the blanket out on a carpeted floor. Let your children take turns hopping from square to square.

**9** Spread a large blanket on the floor. (A blue blanket is perfect for this activity, but any color will work.) Have your children sit around the blanket and grab it with both hands. Show them how to move their hands up and down to make ripples in the blanket "water."

**10** Give each of your children one or two small blankets, such as doll blankets or infant receiving blankets. Have them wave their blankets in the air, down near the ground, and from side to side.

# Riding Toys

**1** Riding toys for toddlers must be small and simple. At this age, riding toys that a child can sit on and push with his or her feet are better than those with pedals.

**2** Toddlers enjoy using riding toys inside and outside. It is helpful to have several of different types so your children will not have to wait very long for a turn. Taking turns and waiting is so difficult for this age group.

**3** In addition to having plenty of riding toys, try this technique for helping your children take turns. Play music while they are using the riding toys. Let them know that whenever a song ends, the children on the riding toys must give the other children their turns.

**4** Wagons are a favorite toy for toddlers. They love to fill wagons with other toys and pull them around the playground. Choose wagons that are small and lightweight for this purpose.

**5** To encourage coordination skills, make a wagon track on the floor with masking tape (or outside on the sidewalk with chalk). Have your children pull or push their wagons along the path.

**6** Children also enjoy riding in a wagon. This kind of wagon should be larger and very sturdy. Toddlers love to be taken for a spin around the playground, waving "bye-bye" to everyone.

**7** In warm weather, toddlers enjoy having a "car wash." Bring out buckets of soapy water and rags and let your children wash all of the riding toys. Provide towels so they can dry their vehicles before riding on them again.

**8** Set up a course for children on riding toys to follow. Use small, plastic orange cones, 2-liter bottles filled with sand, or other markers. Help the children "drive" in the same direction to avoid crashes.

**9** You can also make a racetrack indoors by placing strips of masking tape on the floor about 2 feet apart. Make the track simple or complicated, according to your children's skills. Let the children scoot their riding toys along the track. Encourage them to stay inside the track as much as possible.

**10** Your children will love this tunnel. Cut off both ends of a large cardboard appliance box. Reinforce the box by wrapping tape around its sides. Let your children scoot their riding toys through the tunnel.

# Swings and Slides

**3** Toddlers enjoy putting toys down the slide. Set aside a special time for toys only. Encourage your children to experiment. Which toys roll fast? Which ones roll slowly?

**4** You may find your toddlers hiding under an outdoor slide. This is a great, shady hiding place. It is also fun for them to watch their friends from a different perspective. Watch the children under the slide, cautioning them to keep their hands off the steps and making sure they do not walk right in front of the slide.

**5** Most toddlers will swing as long as you let them. They especially enjoy leaning across a swing and swaying back and forth. A boating bumper hung very low from a swing set works very well for this kind of swinging.

**1** Toddlers need adult supervision whenever they are playing on a slide. Stand by as the child climbs up the stairs and then be there to catch each child at the end of the slide.

**2** Have a few simple rules when your children are sliding: Only one child at a time on the slide (one child must be completely off the slide before the next child starts climbing the stairs); climb *up* the stairs and slide *down* the slide (no climbing up the slide); always slide down feet first.

**6** Toddlers like tire swings that hold more than one child. This makes swinging a much more social way to play. As you push your children, sing a simple song such as the one below.

*Sung to: "Row, Row, Row Your Boat"*

Swing, swing, swing so high.
Swing up to the sky.
Katie's swinging.
Chloe's swinging.
Mark is swinging by.

*Gayle Bittinger*

**7** A toddler is not coordinated enough to pump a swing. When you put a young child on a swing, remind him or her to hold on tight until the swing stops. (This is very important; some children will just let go of the swing when they are done, even if they are still moving.) Swing the child very slowly at first. As your children's skill and experience increases, gradually push them higher.

**8** Try pushing your toddlers from the front of the swing as well as the back. Younger toddlers will appreciate having an adult in front of them as they swing, especially if they are making the transition from a baby swing to a regular one.

**9** Safety is very important around the swings. Young children will walk in front of a swing without realizing the danger. Always be on the lookout for them. One way to minimize this hazard is to have a clearly defined swinging area. For example, you could put landscape timbers around the swing area and fill it with sand or pea gravel. Teach your children not to walk in that area unless they are going to swing.

**10** Waiting for a turn on a swing is so difficult for young children. One way to help with taking turns is to count pushes. Tell each child that you will push him or her for 20 pushes and then it will be the next child's turn. Or push one child as long as it takes you to sing a particular song. When a child knows that his or her turn will be soon, waiting is a little easier.